DELIVERING
happiness™

A PATH TO
PROFITS, PASSION, AND PURPOSE

TONY HSIEH
CEO, Zappos.com, Inc.

"This book could start a revolution! Tony Hsieh
shows how you can dramatically increase your
own happiness—and success—by increasing the
happiness of those around you."

*Marshall Goldsmith, Thinkers 50 world #1 leadership
thinker and million-selling author of MOJO and What
Got You Here Won't Get You There*

delivering happiness™
a path to profits, passion, and purpose

© 2012 tony hsieh
round table comics
www.roundtablecompanies.com
www.roundtablecomics.com

round table companies
1670 valencia way
mundelein, il 60060, usa
phone: 815-346-2398

executive editor: corey michael blake
post production, digital distribution: david c. cohen
llustration, front cover: rob ten pas
coloring: mike dimotta
interior design/layout, back cover: sunny dimartino
proofreading: rita hess

printed in canada

first edition: feb 2012
10 9 8 7 6 5 4 3 2 1

library of congress cataloging-in-publication data
hsieh, tony
delivering happiness / tony hsieh.—1st ed. p. cm.
isbn: 978-1-6106-6024-2
library of congress control number: 2012931905
1. business economics. 2. leadership. i. title.

DELIVERING happiness™

A PATH TO
PROFITS, PASSION, AND PURPOSE

TONY HSIEH
CEO, Zappos.com, Inc.

"This book illustrates so many of Zappos' core values: It's open and honest, passionate and humble, fun and a little weird. Even if you don't care about business, technology, or shoes, you'll be drawn in by this American tale of how hard work, laziness, talent, and failure blend together to create an extraordinary life. You'll learn a lot about happiness along the way, too. I loved it."

Jonathan Haidt, professor of psychology, University of Virginia, and author of The Happiness Hypothesis: Finding Modern Truth in Ancient Wisdom

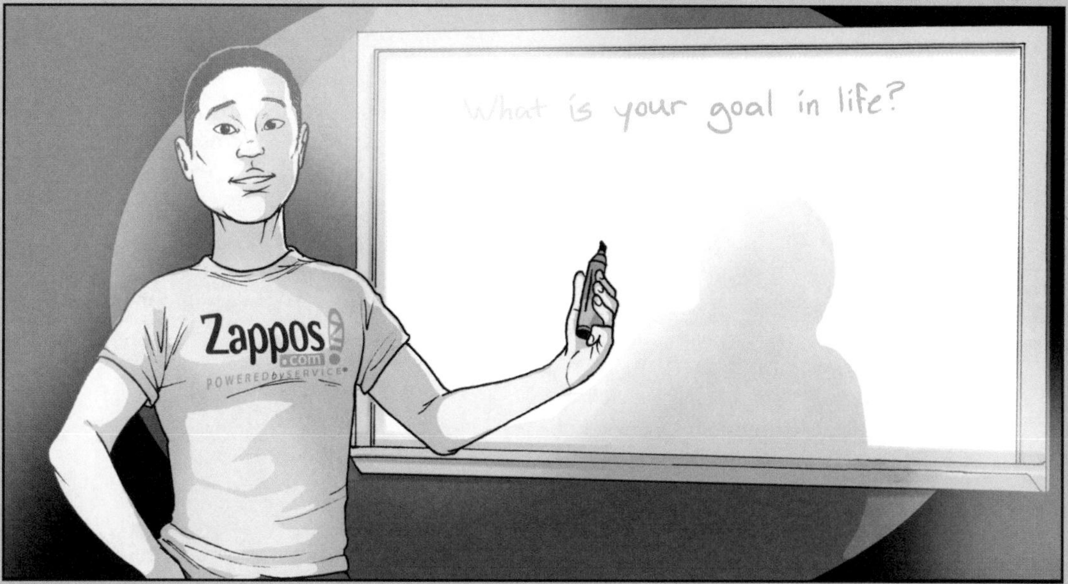
What is your goal in life?
Zappos
.com
POWERED by SERVICE

introduction

Just thinking about the last 18 months since the original version of *Delivering Happiness* arrived in bookstores, it's incredible to see the comic book version of it coming out today (and we've Round Table Companies to thank!).

Many people associate *Delivering Happiness* with Zappos, and rightly so. Zappos was a tremendous part of shaping what *Delivering Happiness,* the Company and the Movement, is today.

With the launch of the *Delivering Happiness* comic book, I thought it'd be the perfect time to update where DH is in our journey. We started from Tony's entrepreneurial stories of raising worms and growing Zappos into a $1 billion company in 10 years. Then we combined the stories and lessons learned in applying (scientific) happiness as a model in business and life. In March 2011, we announced the launch of the company and our movement.

From a scientific sense, research shows that we're super bad at predicting what will give us long-term happiness (ironic, since it's one of the most basic human desires). From a business sense, happier companies prove to be more successful and sustainable in the long-term. From a common, human sense, we can each make the choice to deliver happiness in the world. Whether it's to ourselves, our family and friends, or a complete stranger, research shows that if we deliver happiness, we get happier in return. This is why *Delivering Happiness* exists today. We're here to inspire those day to day choices that will raise happiness levels at work, at home and within our communities around the world.

And to think, it all started on Labor Day, 2009, when Tony and I locked ourselves up in a cabin in Lake Tahoe. We only had a few weeks before our deadline, so we experimented with all sorts of things to keep ourselves as awake and productive as possible. We stocked our cupboards with junk food to reenact our college days of cramming for finals. Tony made chicken soup that he left simmering on the stove until the end of our trip (by then it was so dense, you could stand a knife in it). We tried ingesting all kinds of concoctions—Excedrin, tea, coffee, vodka—even coffee beans in vodka—until our time was up. A couple long weekends later, the book was done.

When the stork dropped *Delivering Happiness* off at bookstores, we didn't know what to expect. Before long, we found out we hit #1 on the *New York Times*, *Wall Street Journal* and Amazon.com best seller lists. It didn't feel real at first, but that changed with one thing: hearing people's responses upon reading it.

On one end, we anticipated business-people reacting to the book (since it was marketed as a business book). But what we didn't expect was the response from the non-business community—people working in education, hospitals, non-profits, and government ... even moms and dads wrote to tell us they were inspired to make a change—big or small—in their lives because of the book.

Then, as the book was translated into different languages, we started hearing from around the world. With every email or story that came in, it felt like a chord had been strum—regardless of background, ethnicity or age—people were not only ready to consider happiness as a model in business and in life, they were ready to do something about it. Even though we didn't know what to expect going in, this reaction was beyond what we ever imagined.

When it came time for the tour, we hit the road on a 23-city, 3-month cross-country bus tour. For us, it was less about selling books, and more about sharing a message we believed in. Again, we didn't know what we were getting into, but we did know this— with every email we got from around the world, and every person we met, we were inspired to do more. This gave birth to the name of our tour (and a mantra we still live by today): **Inspire and Be Inspired.**

After the tour ended, the emails and stories continued to pour in. It was as if we hit a tipping point and we had to do something about it. First it was a book, then it was a bus tour, and now, we're the Delivering Happiness Movement. We've evolved into a company with a cause—to spread and inspire happiness at work, in communities and everyday life.

How are we doing it? With a cool, frosty cup of ICEE:

I – **Inspiration**
C – **Community**
E – **Education**
E – **Experience**

Now we're well on our way to building the DH Family, whether it's:

- **Our growing/inspiring online and offline communities** (in 130 countries, 1200 cities and counting)

- **DH@Work** (our team that helps other companies apply happiness as a business model)

- **DH Shop** (our team that gives everyone a chance to buy something that directly adds to increasing the happiness level in the world)

- **DH@School** (integrating happiness into education) or

- **Content** (to inspire people to be true to themselves, follow their passions and find their higher purpose)

...everything we do comes back to our belief that, together, we can nudge this world to a happier place.

And to think, it's just the beginning. So much has happened in so little time, I can't wait to see where our nudging takes us next.

Jenn
CEO and Chief Happiness Officer
Delivering Happiness

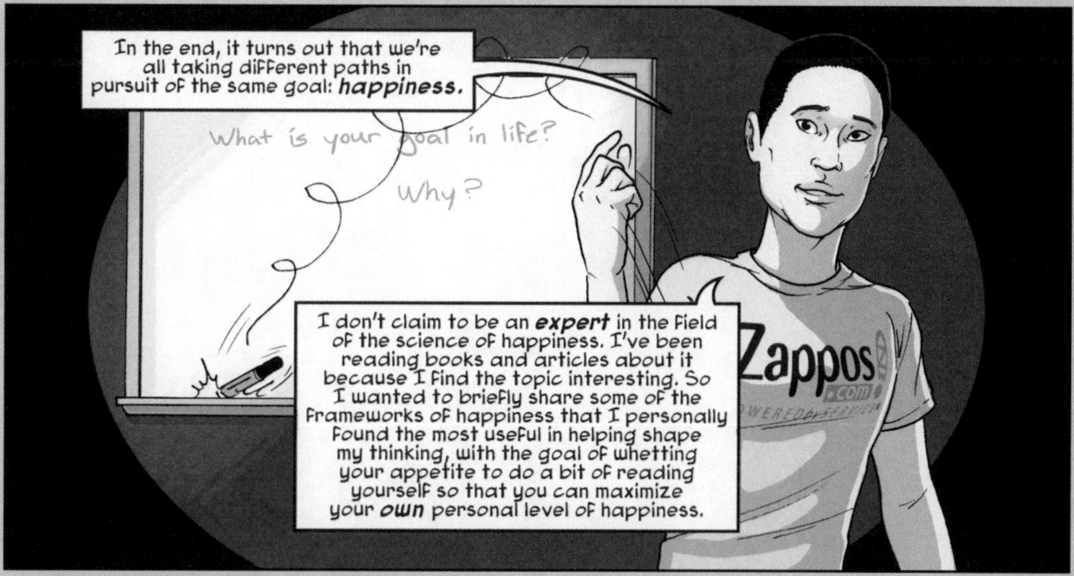
In the end, it turns out that we're all taking different paths in pursuit of the same goal: ***happiness.***
What is your goal in life?
Why?
I don't claim to be an ***expert*** in the field of the science of happiness. I've been reading books and articles about it because I find the topic interesting. So I wanted to briefly share some of the frameworks of happiness that I personally found the most useful in helping shape my thinking, with the goal of whetting your appetite to do a bit of reading yourself so that you can maximize your ***own*** personal level of happiness.
Zappos
.com

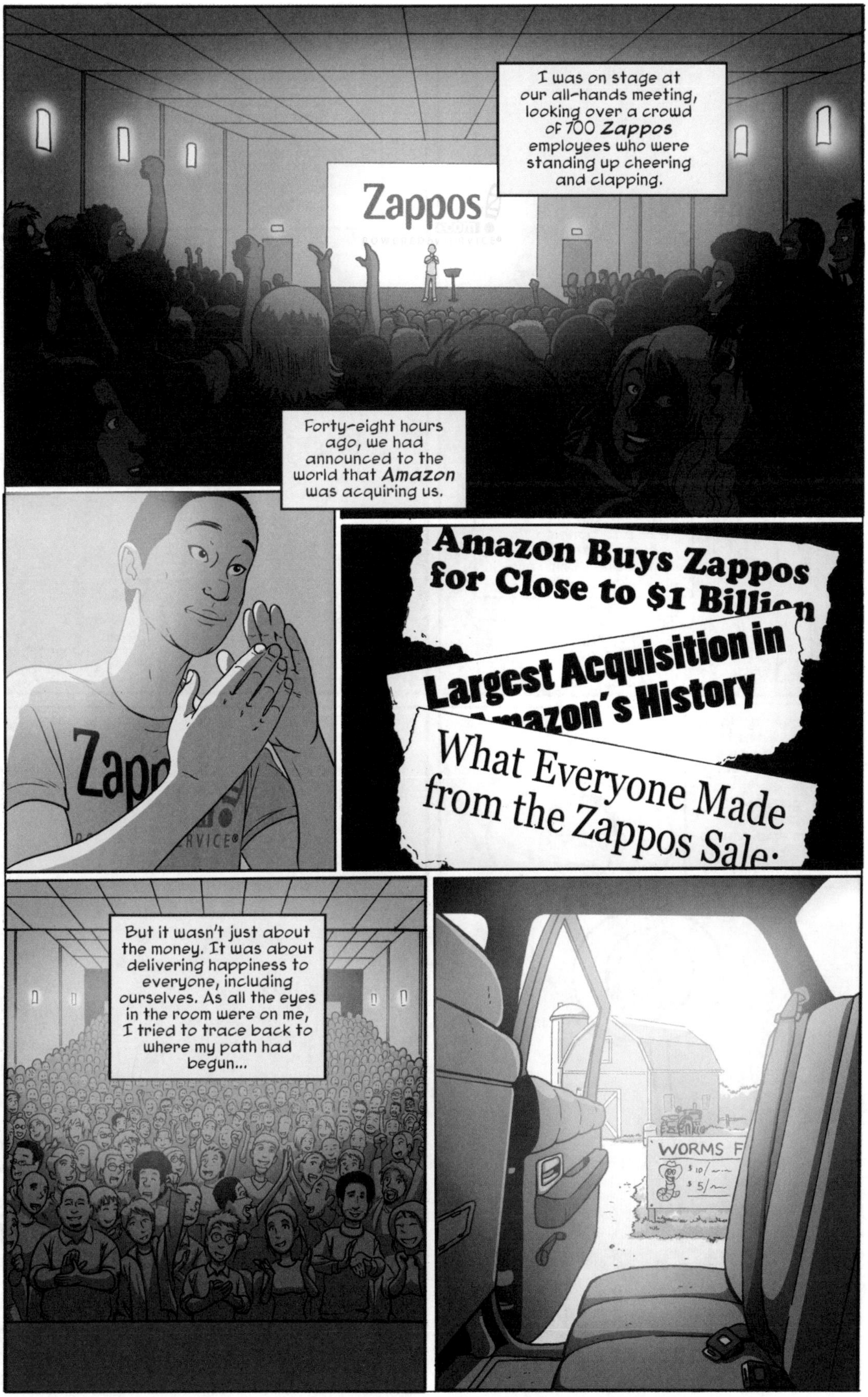
I was on stage at our all-hands meeting, looking over a crowd of 700 *Zappos* employees who were standing up cheering and clapping.
Zappos
Forty-eight hours ago, we had announced to the world that *Amazon* was acquiring us.
Zappos
Amazon Buys Zappos for Close to $1 Billion
Largest Acquisition in Amazon's History
What Everyone Made from the Zappos Sale
But it wasn't just about the money. It was about delivering happiness to everyone, including ourselves. As all the eyes in the room were on me, I tried to trace back to where my path had begun...
WORMS F

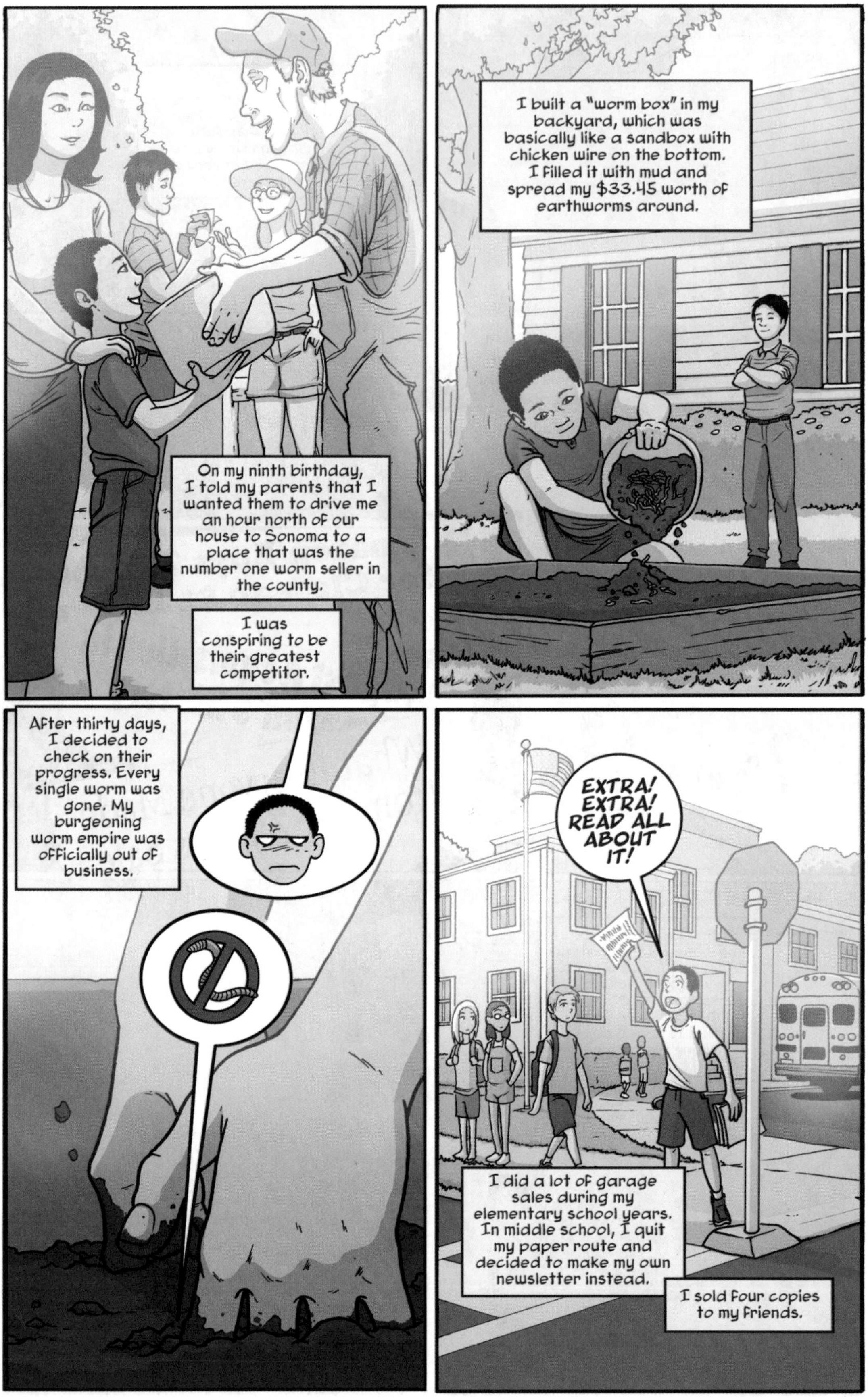
On my ninth birthday, I told my parents that I wanted them to drive me an hour north of our house to Sonoma to a place that was the number one worm seller in the county.
I was conspiring to be their greatest competitor.
I built a "worm box" in my backyard, which was basically like a sandbox with chicken wire on the bottom. I filled it with mud and spread my $33.45 worth of earthworms around.
After thirty days, I decided to check on their progress. Every single worm was gone. My burgeoning worm empire was officially out of business.
EXTRA! EXTRA! READ ALL ABOUT IT!
I did a lot of garage sales during my elementary school years. In middle school, I quit my paper route and decided to make my own newsletter instead.
I sold four copies to my friends.

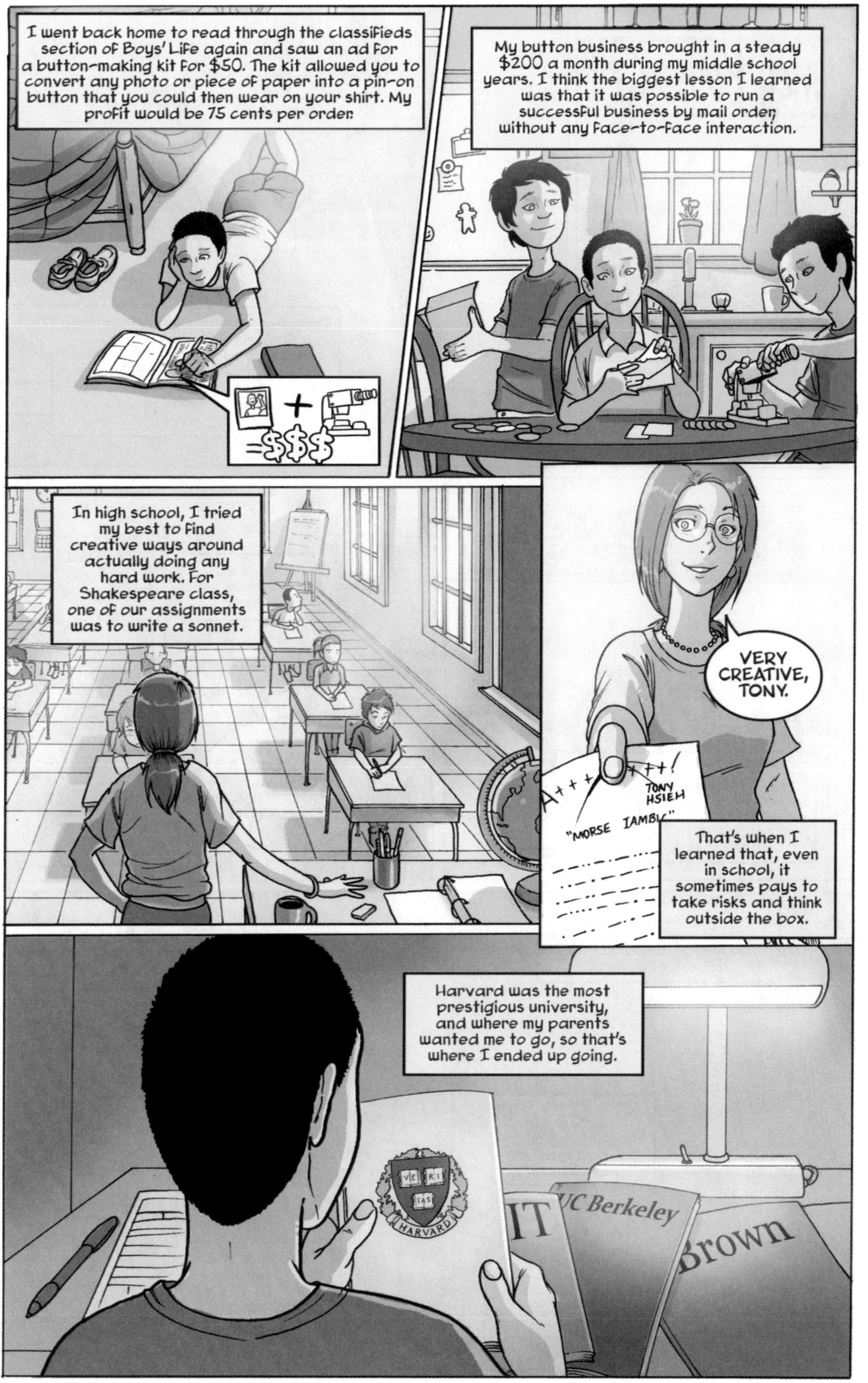
I went back home to read through the classifieds section of Boys' Life again and saw an ad for a button-making kit for $50. The kit allowed you to convert any photo or piece of paper into a pin-on button that you could then wear on your shirt. My profit would be 75 cents per order.
$$$
My button business brought in a steady $200 a month during my middle school years. I think the biggest lesson I learned was that it was possible to run a successful business by mail order, without any face-to-face interaction.
In high school, I tried my best to find creative ways around actually doing any hard work. For Shakespeare class, one of our assignments was to write a sonnet.
VERY CREATIVE, TONY.
TONY HSIEH
That's when I learned that, even in school, it sometimes pays to take risks and think outside the box.
Harvard was the most prestigious university, and where my parents wanted me to go, so that's where I ended up going.
HARVARD
UC Berkeley
Brown

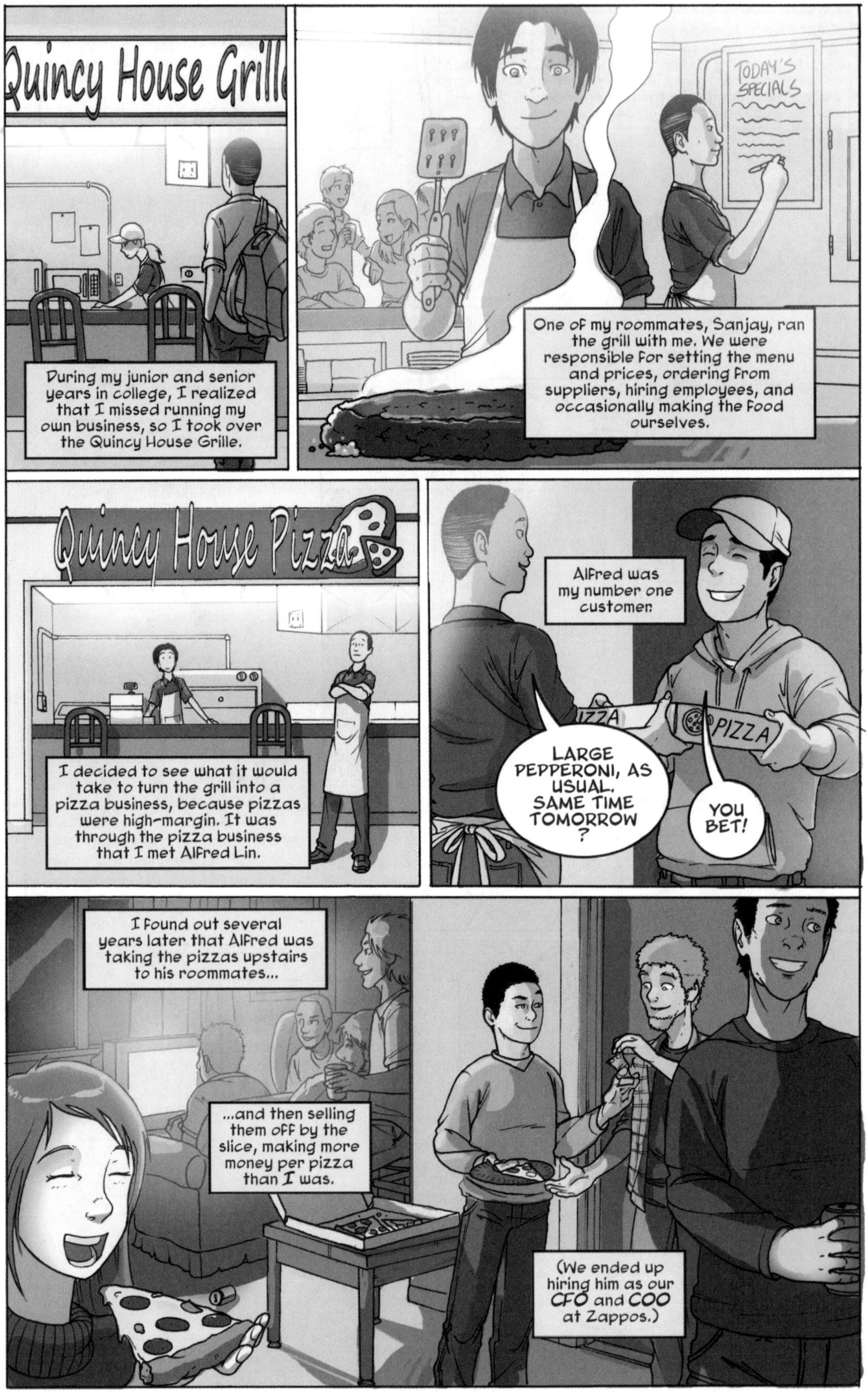
Quincy House Grille
During my junior and senior years in college, I realized that I missed running my own business, so I took over the Quincy House Grille.
TODAY'S SPECIALS
One of my roommates, Sanjay, ran the grill with me. We were responsible for setting the menu and prices, ordering from suppliers, hiring employees, and occasionally making the food ourselves.
Quincy House Pizza
I decided to see what it would take to turn the grill into a pizza business, because pizzas were high-margin. It was through the pizza business that I met Alfred Lin.
Alfred was my number one customer.
PIZZA
LARGE PEPPERONI, AS USUAL. SAME TIME TOMORROW?
YOU BET!
I found out several years later that Alfred was taking the pizzas upstairs to his roommates...
...and then selling them off by the slice, making more money per pizza than I was.
(We ended up hiring him as our CFO and COO at Zappos.)

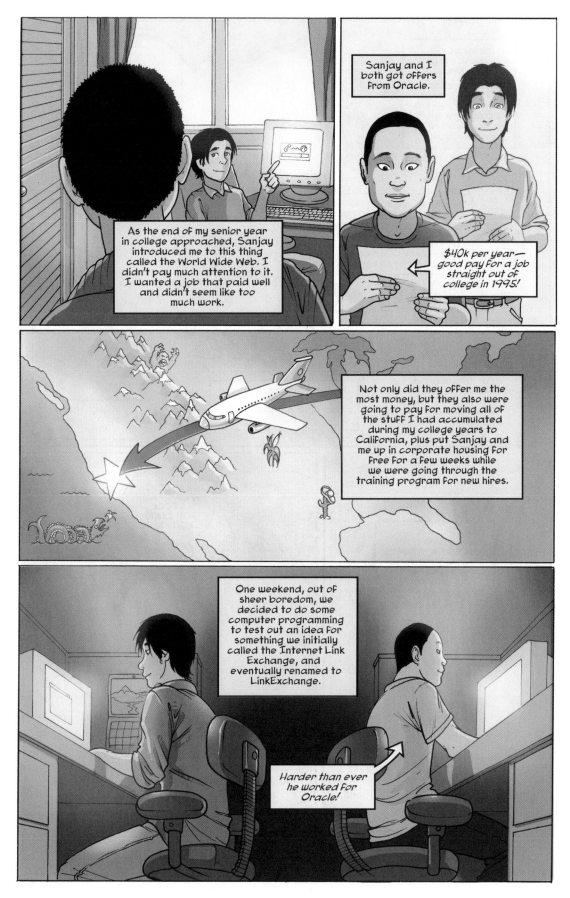

As the end of my senior year in college approached, Sanjay introduced me to this thing called the World Wide Web. I didn't pay much attention to it. I wanted a job that paid well and didn't seem like too much work.

Sanjay and I both got offers from Oracle.

$40k per year—good pay for a job straight out of college in 1995!

Not only did they offer me the most money, but they also were going to pay for moving all of the stuff I had accumulated during my college years to California, plus put Sanjay and me up in corporate housing for free for a few weeks while we were going through the training program for new hires.

One weekend, out of sheer boredom, we decided to do some computer programming to test out an idea for something we initially called the Internet Link Exchange, and eventually renamed to LinkExchange.

Harder than ever he worked for Oracle!

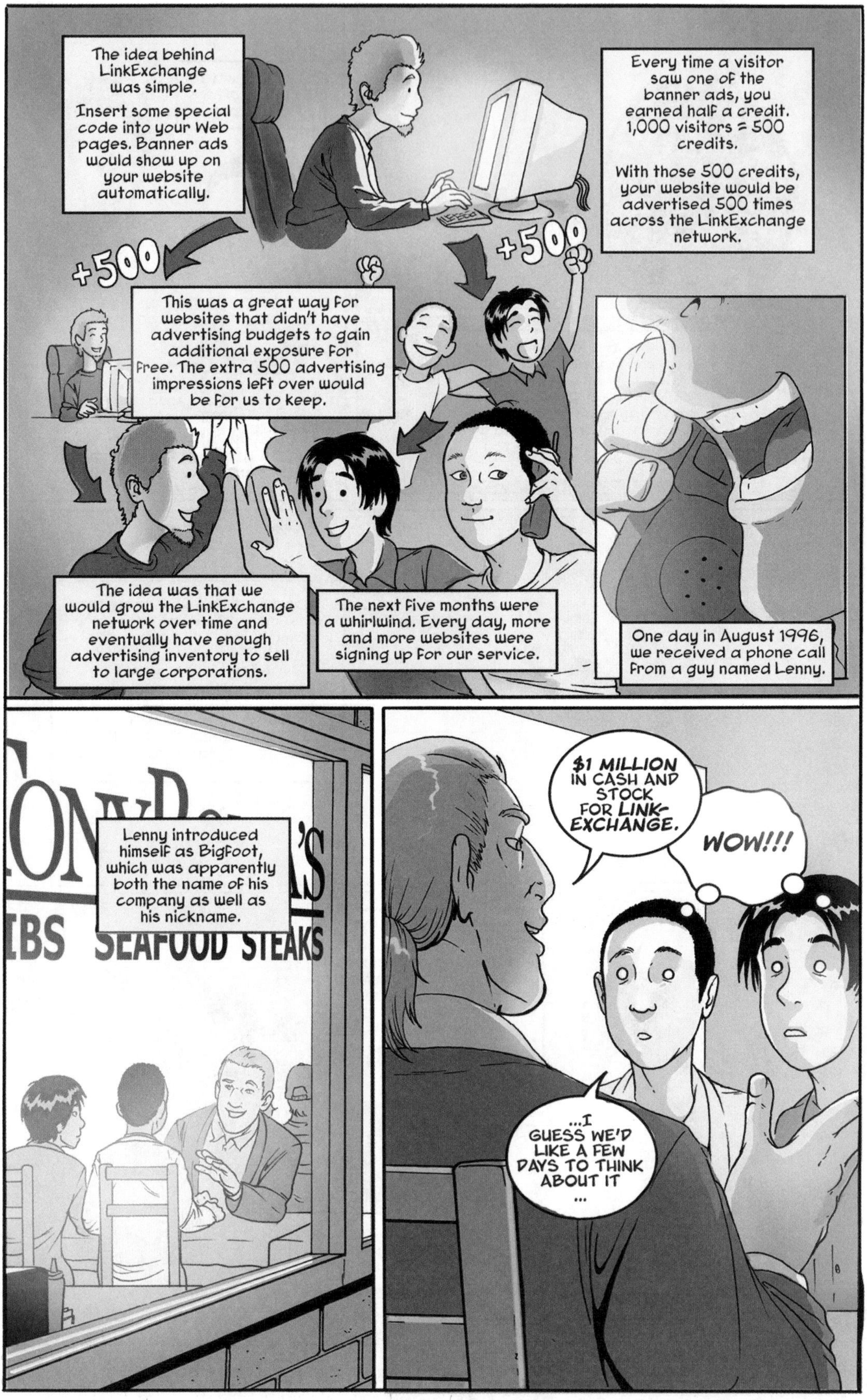

The idea behind LinkExchange was simple.
Insert some special code into your Web pages. Banner ads would show up on your website automatically.
Every time a visitor saw one of the banner ads, you earned half a credit. 1,000 visitors = 500 credits.
With those 500 credits, your website would be advertised 500 times across the LinkExchange network.
+500
+500
This was a great way for websites that didn't have advertising budgets to gain additional exposure for free. The extra 500 advertising impressions left over would be for us to keep.
The idea was that we would grow the LinkExchange network over time and eventually have enough advertising inventory to sell to large corporations.
The next five months were a whirlwind. Every day, more and more websites were signing up for our service.
One day in August 1996, we received a phone call from a guy named Lenny.
Lenny introduced himself as Bigfoot, which was apparently both the name of his company as well as his nickname.
IBS SEAFOOD STEAKS
$1 MILLION IN CASH AND STOCK FOR LINK-EXCHANGE.
WOW!!!
...I GUESS WE'D LIKE A FEW DAYS TO THINK ABOUT IT ...

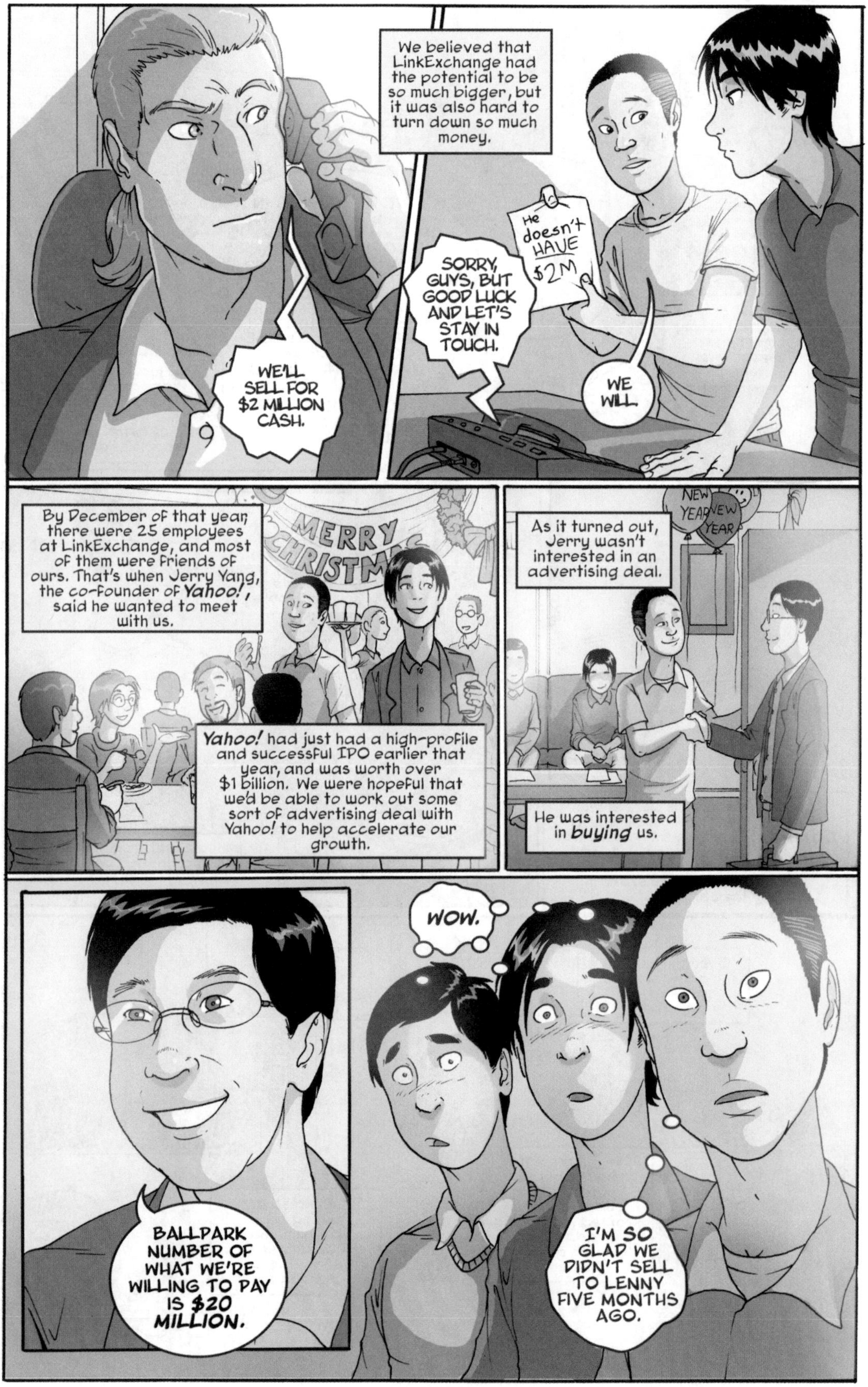
We believed that LinkExchange had the potential to be so much bigger, but it was also hard to turn down so much money.
WE'LL SELL FOR $2 MILLION CASH.
He doesn't HAVE $2M
SORRY, GUYS, BUT GOOD LUCK AND LET'S STAY IN TOUCH.
WE WILL.
By December of that year, there were 25 employees at LinkExchange, and most of them were friends of ours. That's when Jerry Yang, the co-founder of Yahoo!, said he wanted to meet with us.
MERRY CHRISTMAS
Yahoo! had just had a high-profile and successful IPO earlier that year, and was worth over $1 billion. We were hopeful that we'd be able to work out some sort of advertising deal with Yahoo! to help accelerate our growth.
NEW YEAR
NEW YEAR
As it turned out, Jerry wasn't interested in an advertising deal.
He was interested in *buying* us.
BALLPARK NUMBER OF WHAT WE'RE WILLING TO PAY IS $20 MILLION.
WOW.
I'M SO GLAD WE DIDN'T SELL TO LENNY FIVE MONTHS AGO.

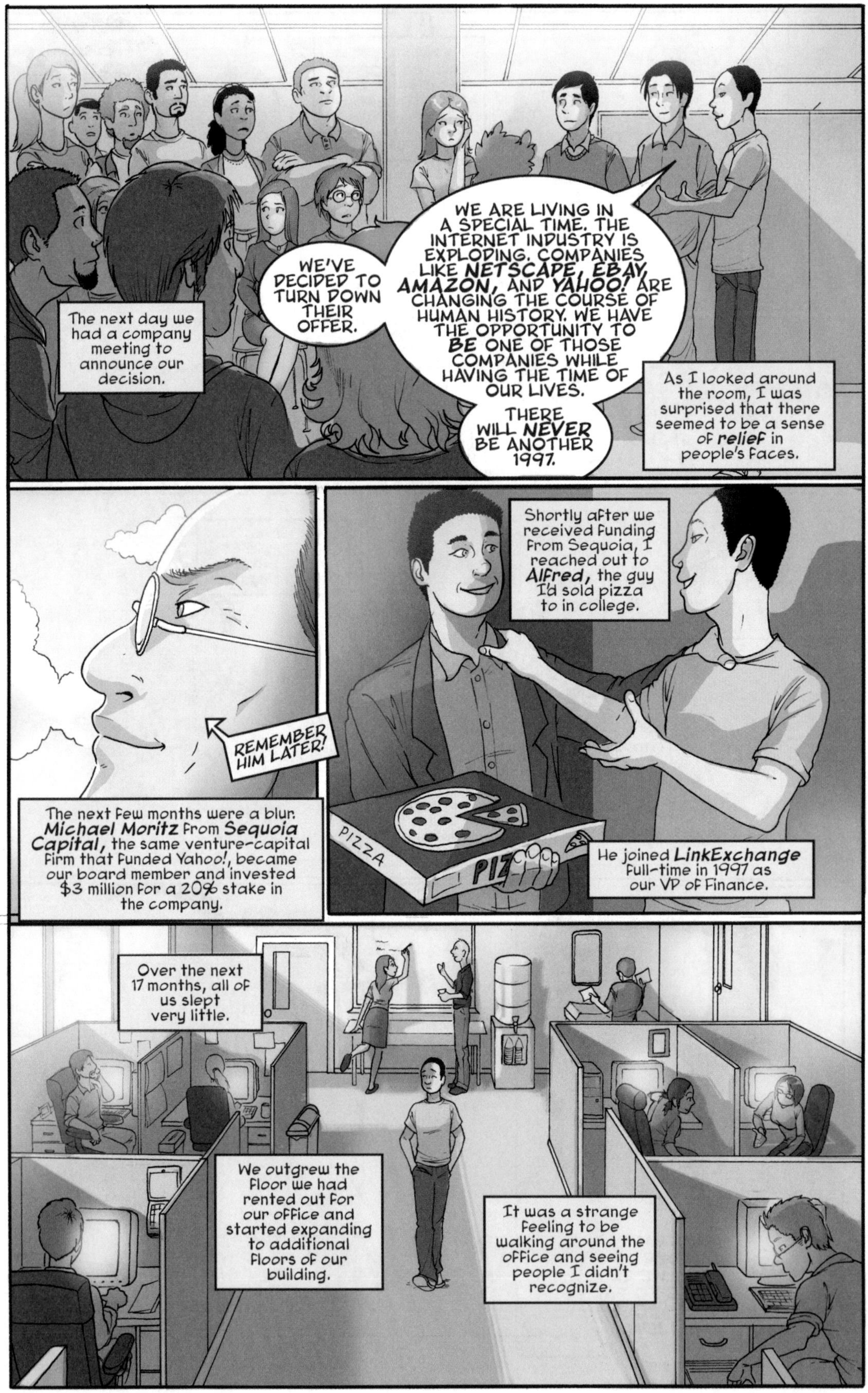
The next day we had a company meeting to announce our decision.
WE'VE DECIDED TO TURN DOWN THEIR OFFER.
WE ARE LIVING IN A SPECIAL TIME. THE INTERNET INDUSTRY IS EXPLODING. COMPANIES LIKE NETSCAPE, EBAY, AMAZON, AND YAHOO! ARE CHANGING THE COURSE OF HUMAN HISTORY. WE HAVE THE OPPORTUNITY TO BE ONE OF THOSE COMPANIES WHILE HAVING THE TIME OF OUR LIVES.
THERE WILL NEVER BE ANOTHER 1997.
As I looked around the room, I was surprised that there seemed to be a sense of relief in people's faces.
REMEMBER HIM LATER!
The next few months were a blur. Michael Moritz from Sequoia Capital, the same venture-capital firm that funded Yahoo!, became our board member and invested $3 million for a 20% stake in the company.
Shortly after we received funding from Sequoia, I reached out to Alfred, the guy I'd sold pizza to in college.
PIZZA
PIZ
He joined LinkExchange full-time in 1997 as our VP of Finance.
Over the next 17 months, all of us slept very little.
We outgrew the floor we had rented out for our office and started expanding to additional floors of our building.
It was a strange feeling to be walking around the office and seeing people I didn't recognize.

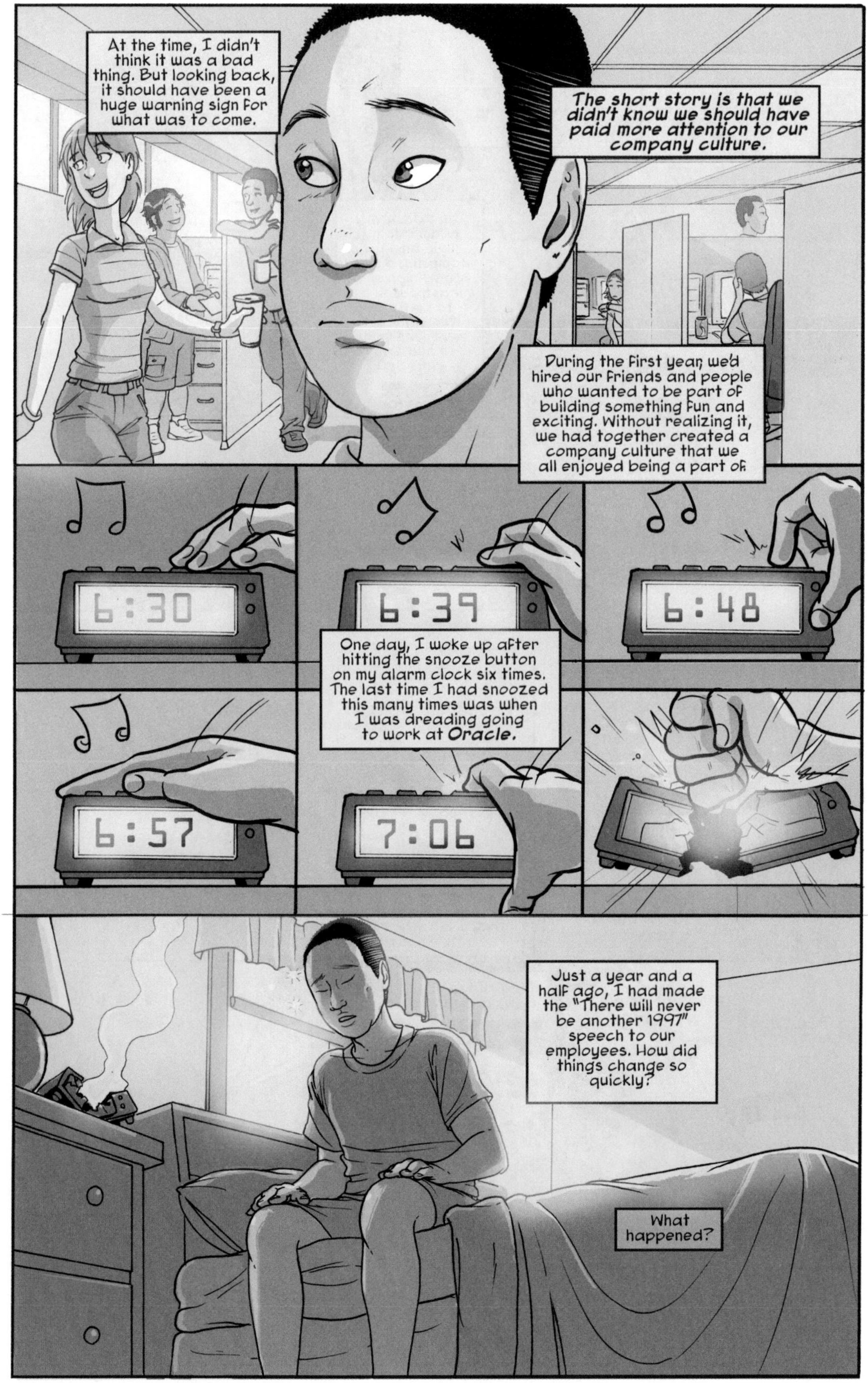
At the time, I didn't think it was a bad thing. But looking back, it should have been a huge warning sign for what was to come.
The short story is that we didn't know we should have paid more attention to our company culture.
During the first year, we'd hired our friends and people who wanted to be part of building something fun and exciting. Without realizing it, we had together created a company culture that we all enjoyed being a part of.
6:30
6:39
6:48
One day, I woke up after hitting the snooze button on my alarm clock six times. The last time I had snoozed this many times was when I was dreading going to work at Oracle.
6:57
7:06
Just a year and a half ago, I had made the "There will never be another 1997" speech to our employees. How did things change so quickly?
What happened?

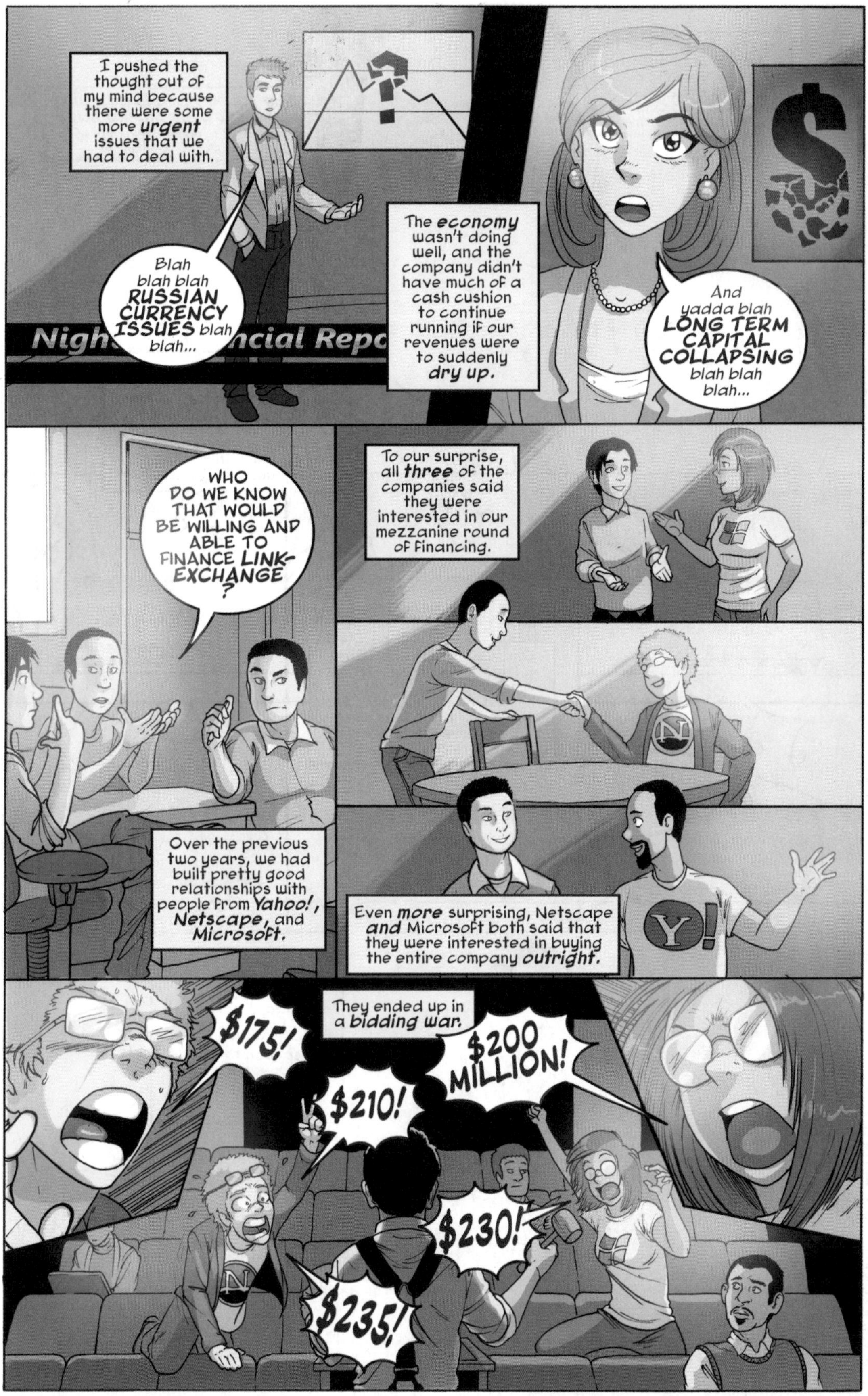
I pushed the thought out of my mind because there were some more urgent issues that we had to deal with.
Blah blah blah RUSSIAN CURRENCY ISSUES blah blah...
The economy wasn't doing well, and the company didn't have much of a cash cushion to continue running if our revenues were to suddenly dry up.
And yadda blah LONG TERM CAPITAL COLLAPSING blah blah blah...
WHO DO WE KNOW THAT WOULD BE WILLING AND ABLE TO FINANCE LINK-EXCHANGE?
Over the previous two years, we had built pretty good relationships with people from Yahoo!, Netscape, and Microsoft.
To our surprise, all three of the companies said they were interested in our mezzanine round of financing.
Even more surprising, Netscape and Microsoft both said that they were interested in buying the entire company outright.
They ended up in a bidding war.
$175!
$200 MILLION!
$210!
$230!
$235!

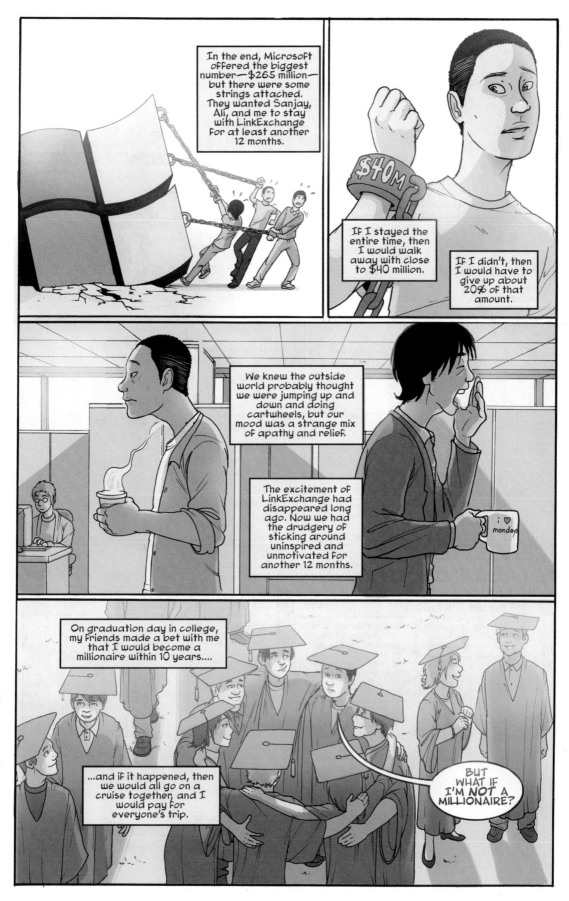

In the end, Microsoft offered the biggest number—$265 million—but there were some strings attached. They wanted Sanjay, Ali, and me to stay with LinkExchange for at least another 12 months.

If I stayed the entire time, then I would walk away with close to $40 million.

If I didn't, then I would have to give up about 20% of that amount.

We knew the outside world probably thought we were jumping up and down and doing cartwheels, but our mood was a strange mix of apathy and relief.

The excitement of LinkExchange had disappeared long ago. Now we had the drudgery of sticking around uninspired and unmotivated for another 12 months.

On graduation day in college, my friends made a bet with me that I would become a millionaire within 10 years....

...and if it happened, then we would all go on a cruise together, and I would pay for everyone's trip.

BUT WHAT IF I'M **NOT** A MILLIONAIRE?

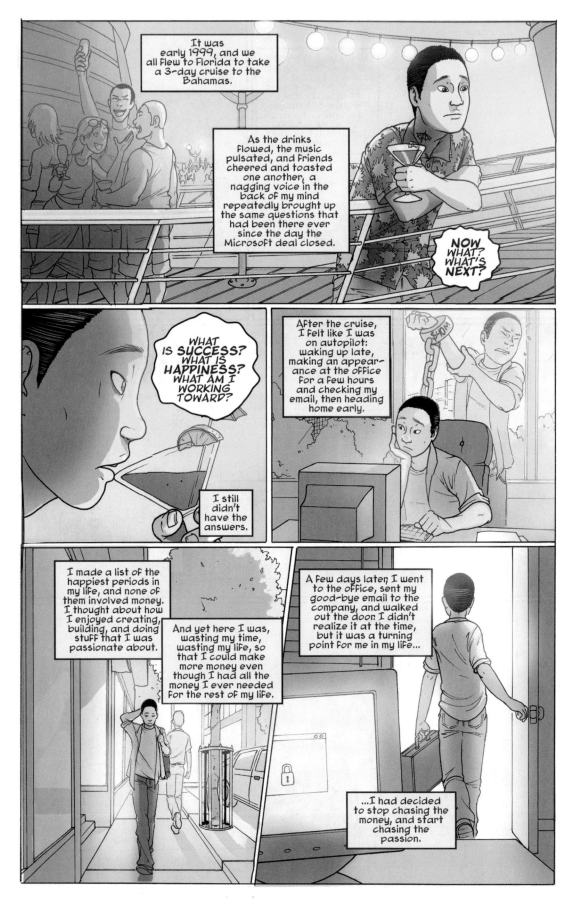

It was early 1999, and we all flew to Florida to take a 3-day cruise to the Bahamas.

As the drinks flowed, the music pulsated, and friends cheered and toasted one another, a nagging voice in the back of my mind repeatedly brought up the same questions that had been there ever since the day the Microsoft deal closed.

NOW WHAT? WHAT'S NEXT?

WHAT IS SUCCESS? WHAT IS HAPPINESS? WHAT AM I WORKING TOWARD?

I still didn't have the answers.

After the cruise, I felt like I was on autopilot: waking up late, making an appearance at the office for a few hours and checking my email, then heading home early.

I made a list of the happiest periods in my life, and none of them involved money. I thought about how I enjoyed creating, building, and doing stuff that I was passionate about.

And yet here I was, wasting my time, wasting my life, so that I could make more money even though I had all the money I ever needed for the rest of my life.

A few days later, I went to the office, sent my good-bye email to the company, and walked out the door. I didn't realize it at the time, but it was a turning point for me in my life...

...I had decided to stop chasing the money, and start chasing the passion.

12

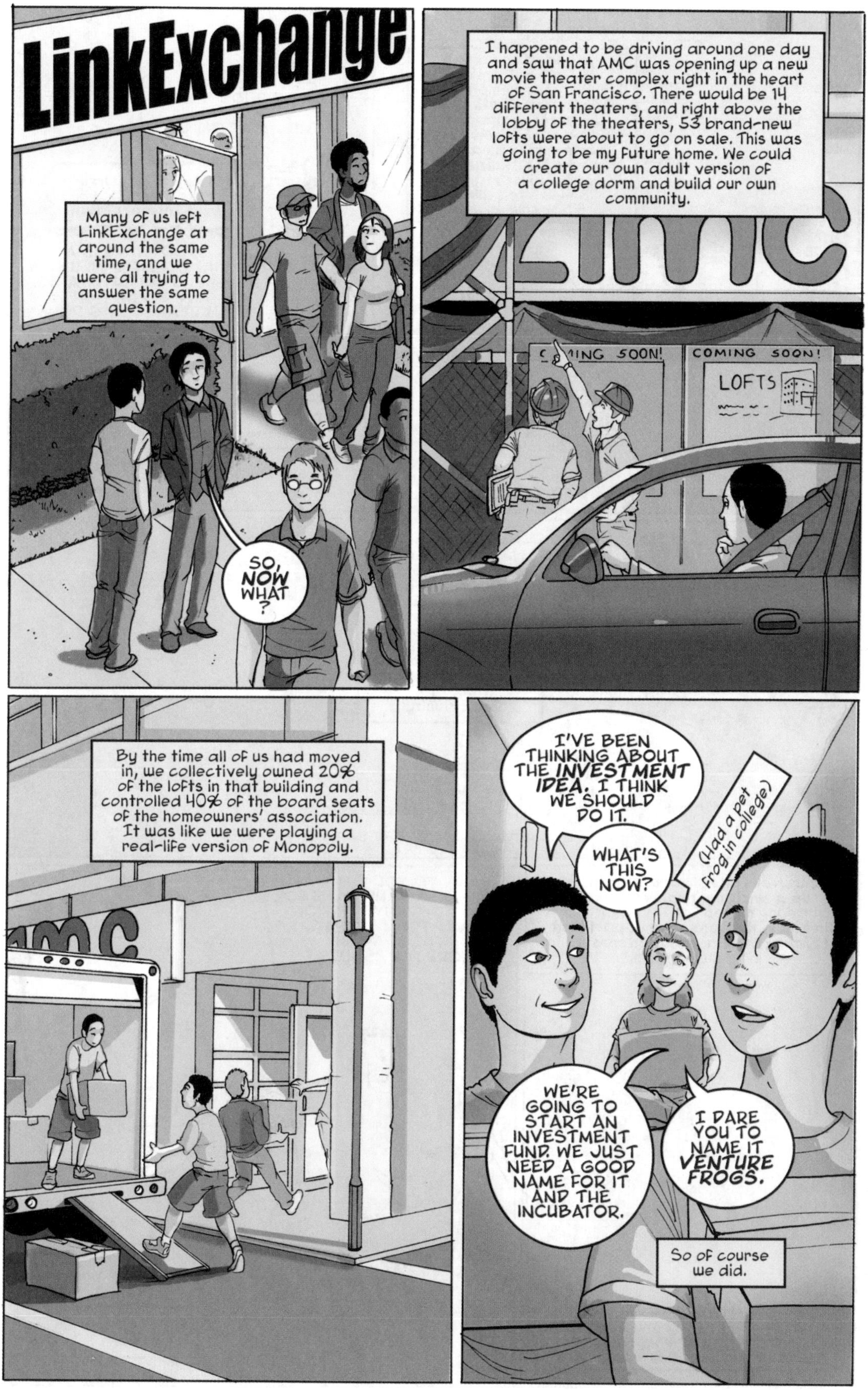

LinkExchange
Many of us left LinkExchange at around the same time, and we were all trying to answer the same question.
SO, NOW WHAT?
I happened to be driving around one day and saw that AMC was opening up a new movie theater complex right in the heart of San Francisco. There would be 14 different theaters, and right above the lobby of the theaters, 53 brand-new lofts were about to go on sale. This was going to be my future home. We could create our own adult version of a college dorm and build our own community.
COMING SOON!
LOFTS
By the time all of us had moved in, we collectively owned 20% of the lofts in that building and controlled 40% of the board seats of the homeowners' association. It was like we were playing a real-life version of Monopoly.
I'VE BEEN THINKING ABOUT THE INVESTMENT IDEA. I THINK WE SHOULD DO IT.
WHAT'S THIS NOW?
(Had a pet frog in college)
WE'RE GOING TO START AN INVESTMENT FUND. WE JUST NEED A GOOD NAME FOR IT AND THE INCUBATOR.
I DARE YOU TO NAME IT VENTURE FROGS.
So of course we did.

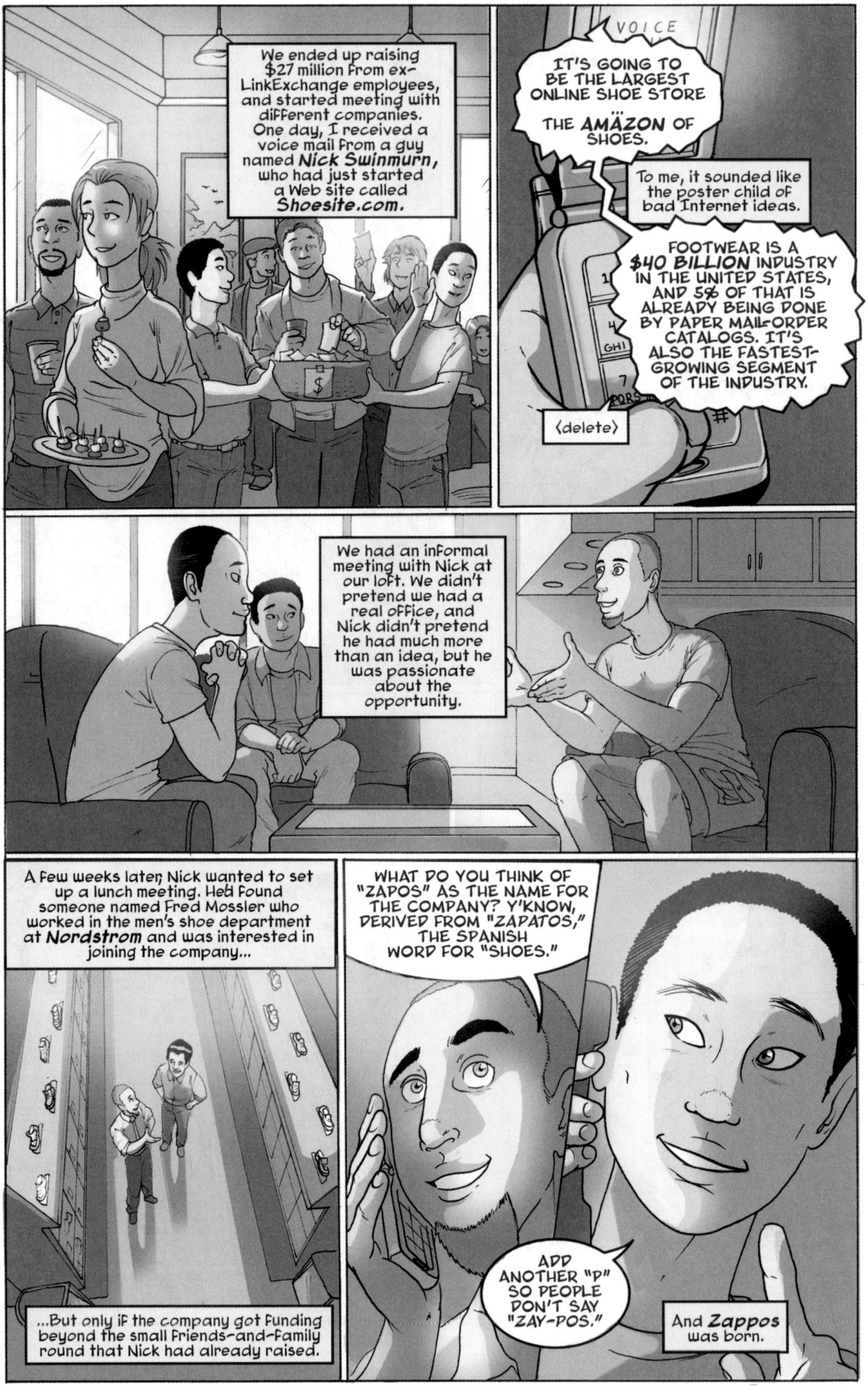
We ended up raising $27 million from ex-LinkExchange employees, and started meeting with different companies. One day, I received a voice mail from a guy named Nick Swinmurn, who had just started a Web site called Shoesite.com.
VOICE
IT'S GOING TO BE THE LARGEST ONLINE SHOE STORE ... THE AMAZON OF SHOES.
To me, it sounded like the poster child of bad Internet ideas.
FOOTWEAR IS A $40 BILLION INDUSTRY IN THE UNITED STATES, AND 5% OF THAT IS ALREADY BEING DONE BY PAPER MAIL-ORDER CATALOGS. IT'S ALSO THE FASTEST-GROWING SEGMENT OF THE INDUSTRY.
(delete)
We had an informal meeting with Nick at our loft. We didn't pretend we had a real office, and Nick didn't pretend he had much more than an idea, but he was passionate about the opportunity.
A few weeks later, Nick wanted to set up a lunch meeting. He'd found someone named Fred Mossler who worked in the men's shoe department at Nordstrom and was interested in joining the company...
...But only if the company got funding beyond the small friends-and-family round that Nick had already raised.
WHAT DO YOU THINK OF "ZAPOS" AS THE NAME FOR THE COMPANY? Y'KNOW, DERIVED FROM "ZAPATOS," THE SPANISH WORD FOR "SHOES."
ADD ANOTHER "P" SO PEOPLE DON'T SAY "ZAY-POS."
And Zappos was born.

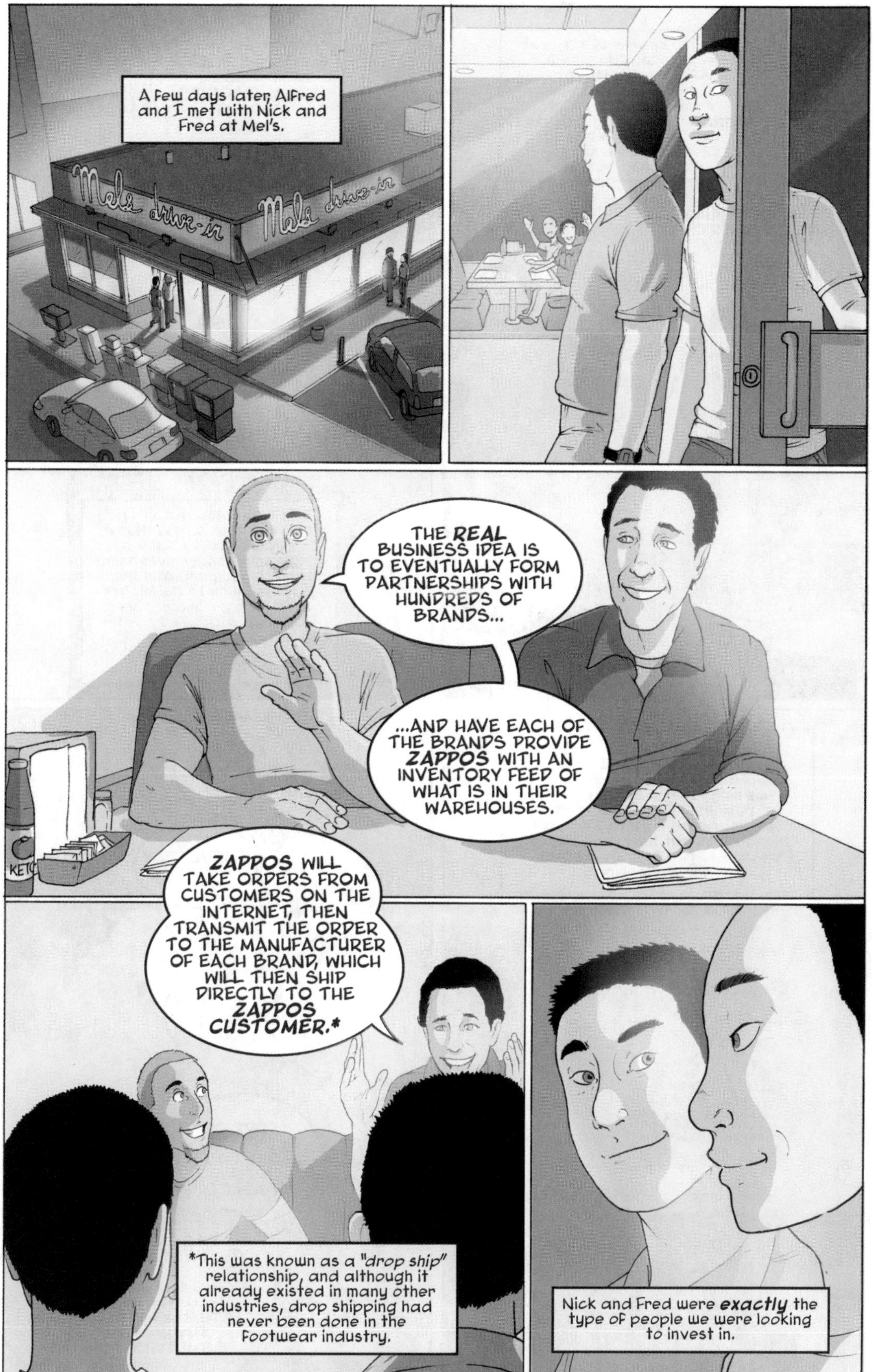

A few days later, Alfred and I met with Nick and Fred at Mel's.
Mel's drive-in
Mel's drive-in
THE REAL BUSINESS IDEA IS TO EVENTUALLY FORM PARTNERSHIPS WITH HUNDREDS OF BRANDS...
...AND HAVE EACH OF THE BRANDS PROVIDE ZAPPOS WITH AN INVENTORY FEED OF WHAT IS IN THEIR WAREHOUSES.
ZAPPOS WILL TAKE ORDERS FROM CUSTOMERS ON THE INTERNET, THEN TRANSMIT THE ORDER TO THE MANUFACTURER OF EACH BRAND, WHICH WILL THEN SHIP DIRECTLY TO THE ZAPPOS CUSTOMER.*
*This was known as a "drop ship" relationship, and although it already existed in many other industries, drop shipping had never been done in the footwear industry.
Nick and Fred were exactly the type of people we were looking to invest in.

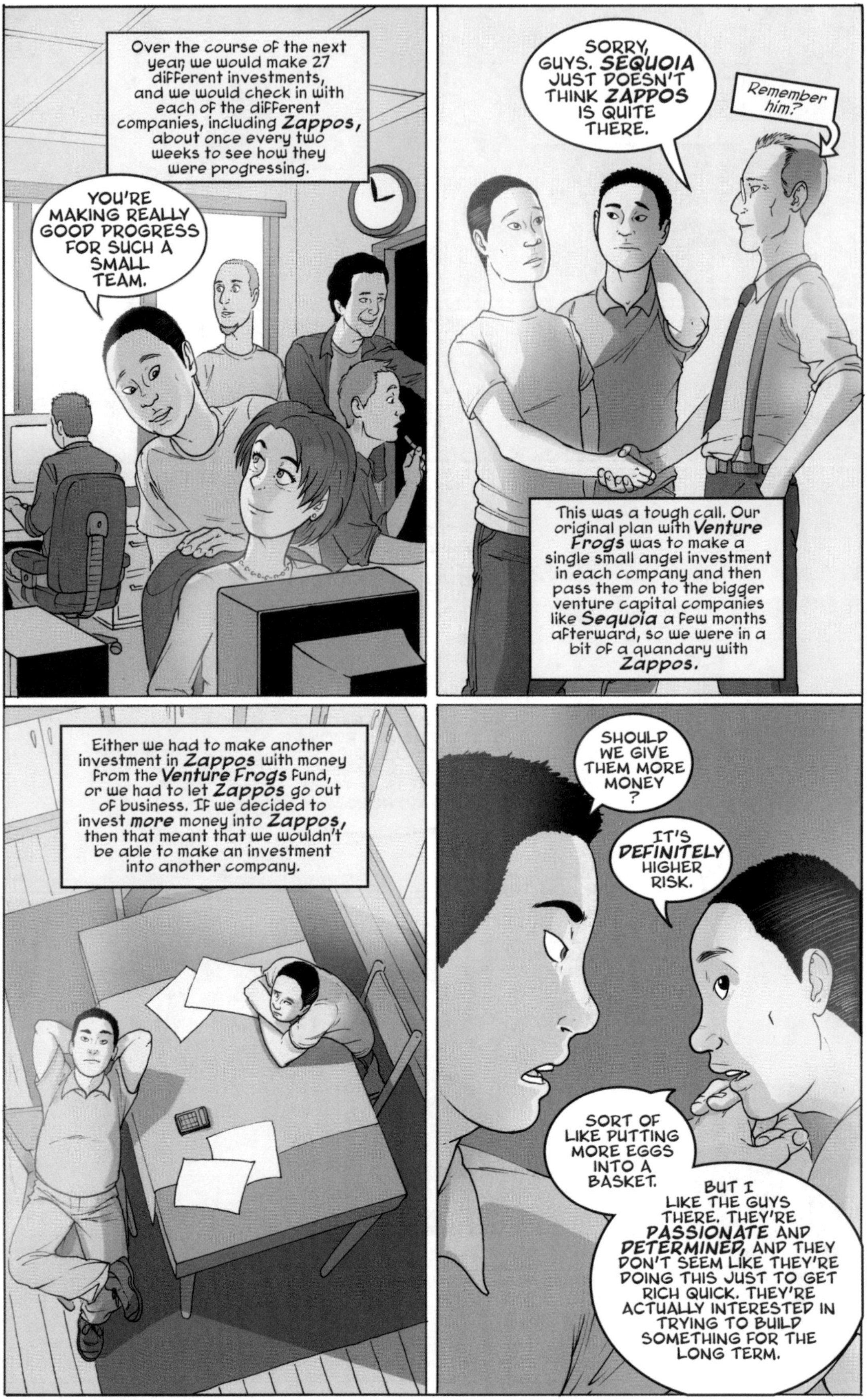
Over the course of the next year, we would make 27 different investments, and we would check in with each of the different companies, including Zappos, about once every two weeks to see how they were progressing.
YOU'RE MAKING REALLY GOOD PROGRESS FOR SUCH A SMALL TEAM.
SORRY, GUYS. SEQUOIA JUST DOESN'T THINK ZAPPOS IS QUITE THERE.
Remember him?
This was a tough call. Our original plan with Venture Frogs was to make a single small angel investment in each company and then pass them on to the bigger venture capital companies like Sequoia a few months afterward, so we were in a bit of a quandary with Zappos.
Either we had to make another investment in Zappos with money from the Venture Frogs fund, or we had to let Zappos go out of business. If we decided to invest more money into Zappos, then that meant that we wouldn't be able to make an investment into another company.
SHOULD WE GIVE THEM MORE MONEY?
IT'S DEFINITELY HIGHER RISK.
SORT OF LIKE PUTTING MORE EGGS INTO A BASKET.
BUT I LIKE THE GUYS THERE. THEY'RE PASSIONATE AND DETERMINED, AND THEY DON'T SEEM LIKE THEY'RE DOING THIS JUST TO GET RICH QUICK. THEY'RE ACTUALLY INTERESTED IN TRYING TO BUILD SOMETHING FOR THE LONG TERM.

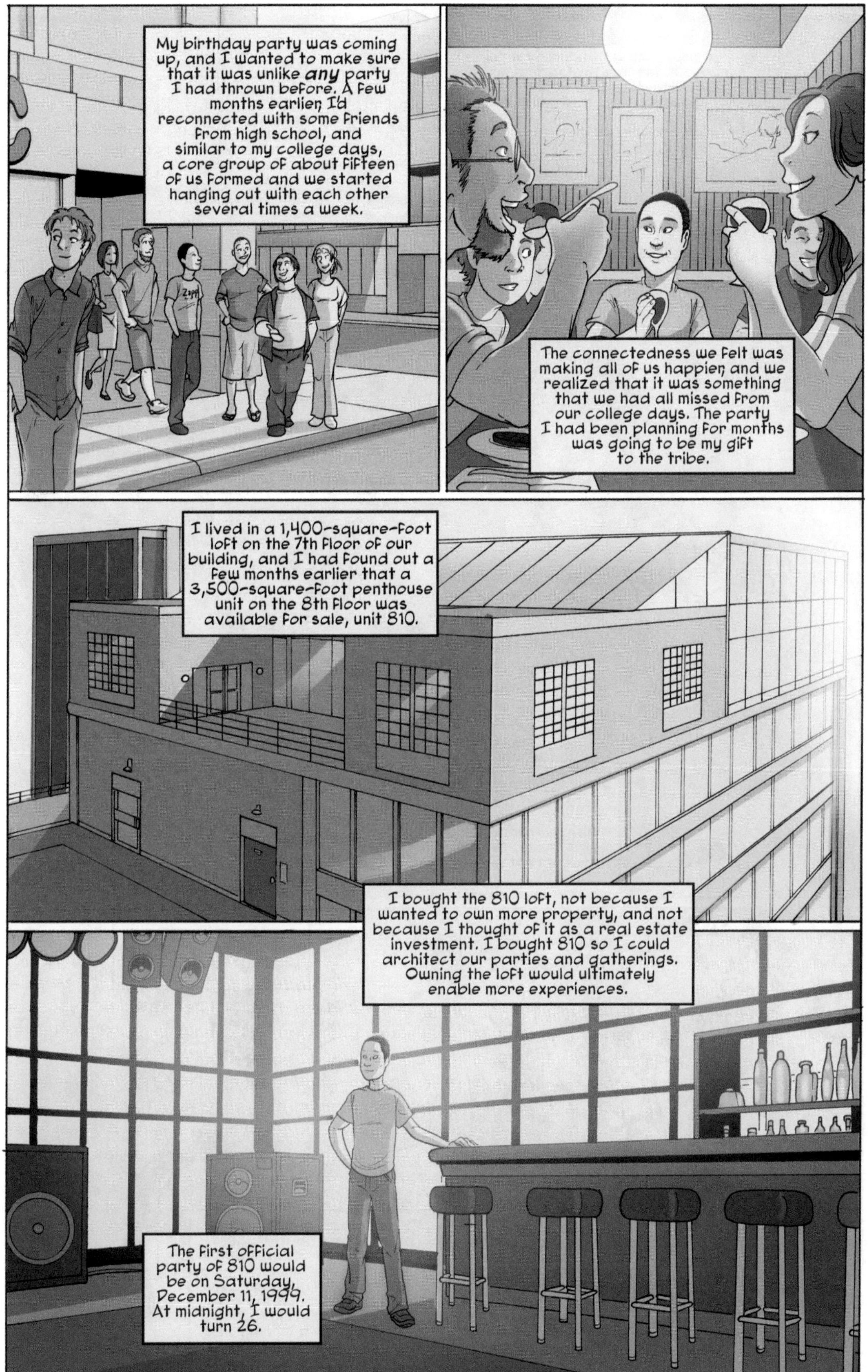
My birthday party was coming up, and I wanted to make sure that it was unlike *any* party I had thrown before. A few months earlier, I'd reconnected with some friends from high school, and similar to my college days, a core group of about fifteen of us formed and we started hanging out with each other several times a week.
The connectedness we felt was making all of us happier, and we realized that it was something that we had all missed from our college days. The party I had been planning for months was going to be my gift to the tribe.
I lived in a 1,400-square-foot loft on the 7th floor of our building, and I had found out a few months earlier that a 3,500-square-foot penthouse unit on the 8th floor was available for sale, unit 810.
I bought the 810 loft, not because I wanted to own more property, and not because I thought of it as a real estate investment. I bought 810 so I could architect our parties and gatherings. Owning the loft would ultimately enable more experiences.
The first official party of 810 would be on Saturday, December 11, 1999. At midnight, I would turn 26.

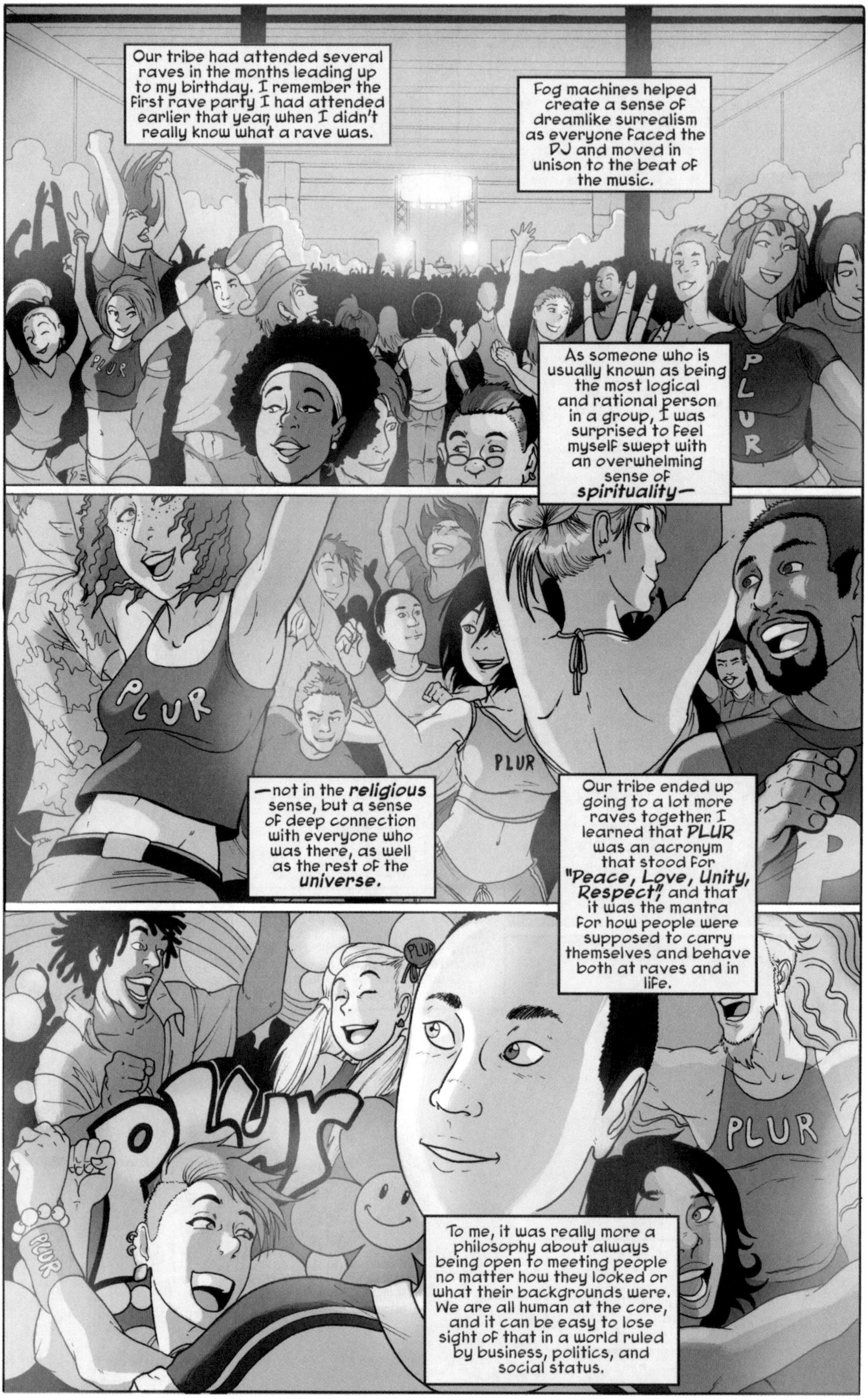
Our tribe had attended several raves in the months leading up to my birthday. I remember the first rave party I had attended earlier that year, when I didn't really know what a rave was.
Fog machines helped create a sense of dreamlike surrealism as everyone faced the DJ and moved in unison to the beat of the music.
PLUR
PLUR
As someone who is usually known as being the most logical and rational person in a group, I was surprised to feel myself swept with an overwhelming sense of spirituality—
PLUR
PLUR
—not in the religious sense, but a sense of deep connection with everyone who was there, as well as the rest of the universe.
Our tribe ended up going to a lot more raves together. I learned that PLUR was an acronym that stood for "Peace, Love, Unity, Respect," and that it was the mantra for how people were supposed to carry themselves and behave both at raves and in life.
PLUR
PLUR
PLUR
PLUR
To me, it was really more a philosophy about always being open to meeting people no matter how they looked or what their backgrounds were. We are all human at the core, and it can be easy to lose sight of that in a world ruled by business, politics, and social status.

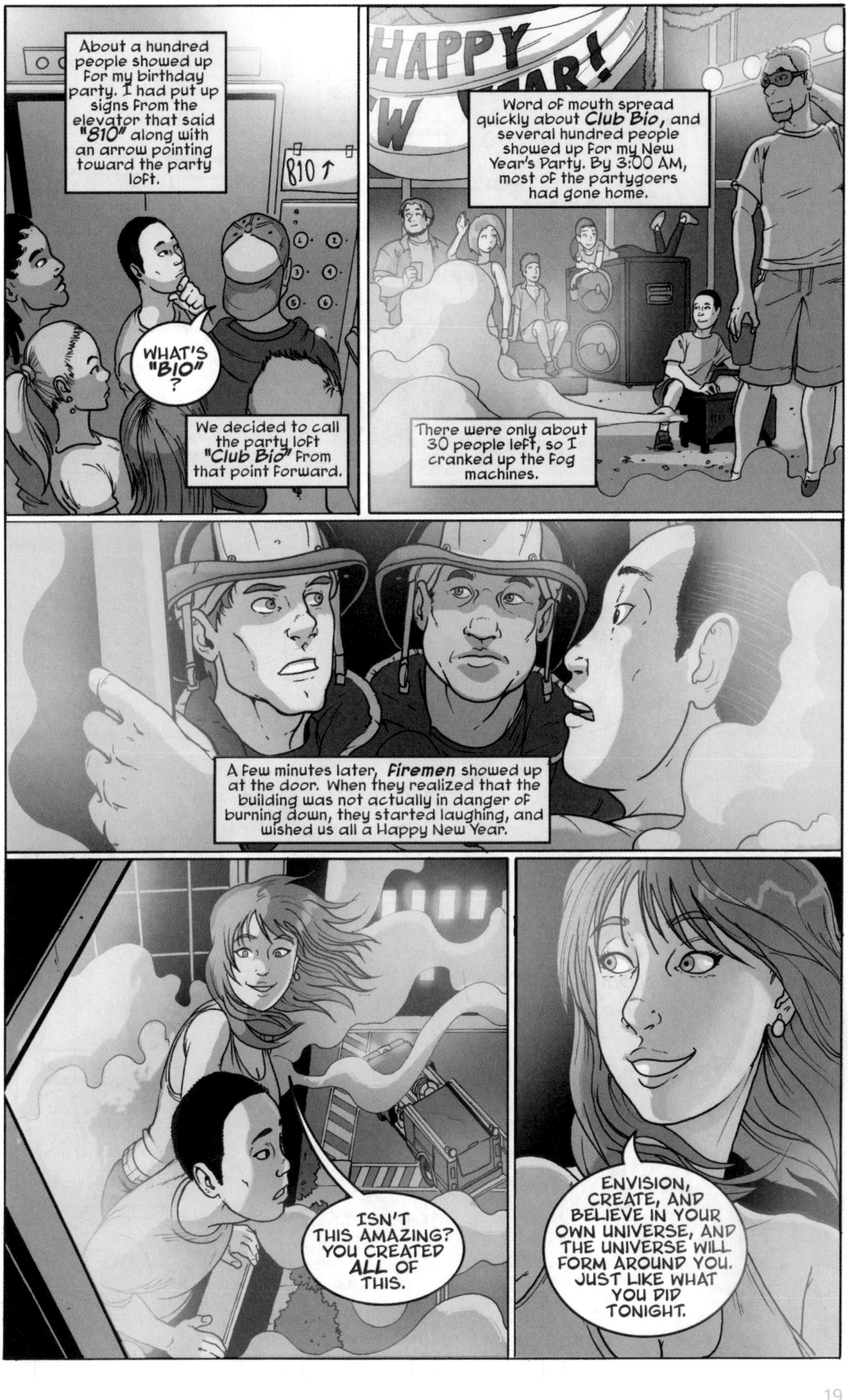
About a hundred people showed up for my birthday party. I had put up signs from the elevator that said "810" along with an arrow pointing toward the party loft.
810 ↑
WHAT'S "BIO"?
We decided to call the party loft "Club Bio" from that point forward.
HAPPY NEW YEAR!
Word of mouth spread quickly about Club Bio, and several hundred people showed up for my New Year's Party. By 3:00 AM, most of the partygoers had gone home.
There were only about 30 people left, so I cranked up the fog machines.
A few minutes later, firemen showed up at the door. When they realized that the building was not actually in danger of burning down, they started laughing, and wished us all a Happy New Year.
ISN'T THIS AMAZING? YOU CREATED ALL OF THIS.
ENVISION, CREATE, AND BELIEVE IN YOUR OWN UNIVERSE, AND THE UNIVERSE WILL FORM AROUND YOU. JUST LIKE WHAT YOU DID TONIGHT.

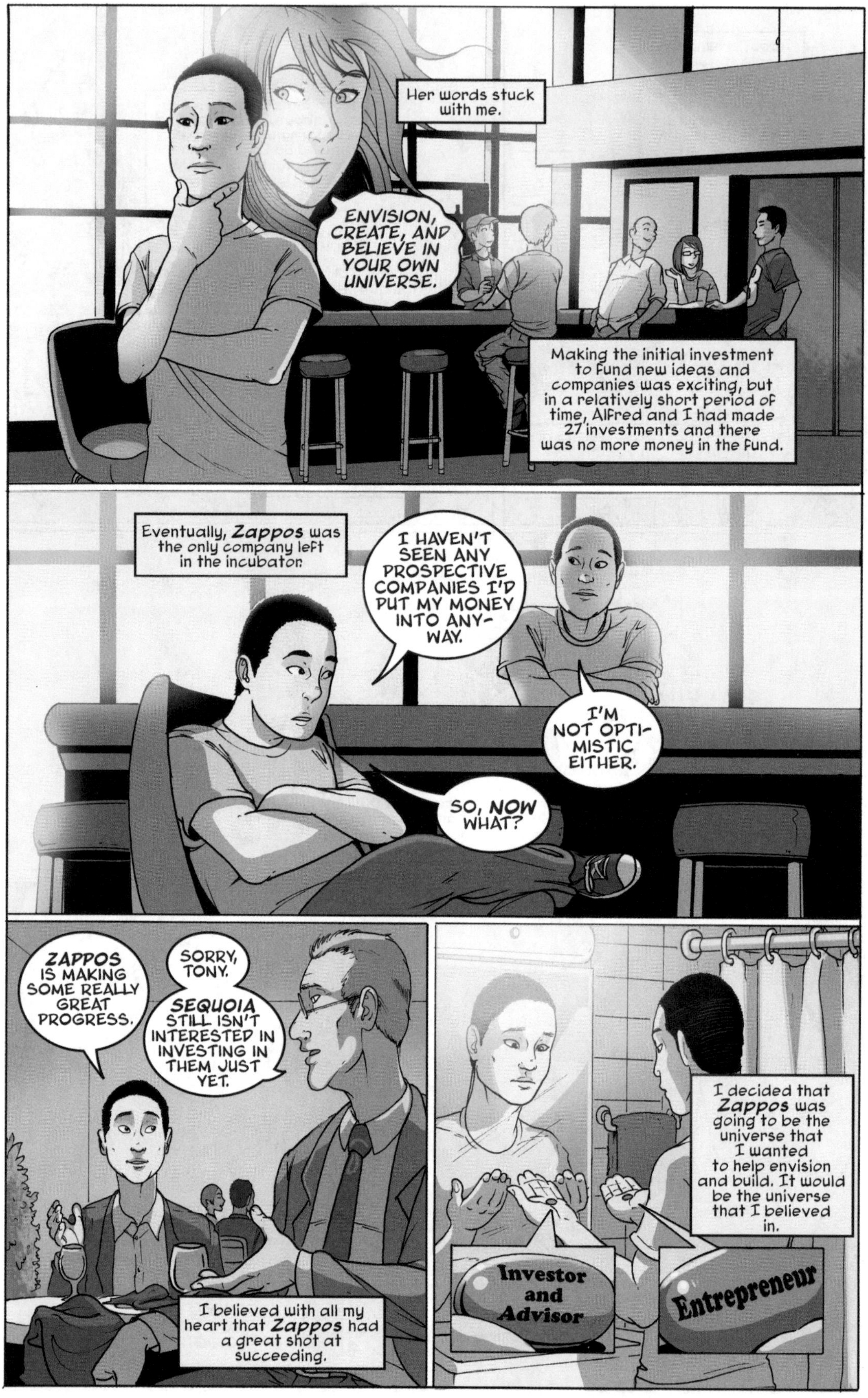
Her words stuck with me.
ENVISION, CREATE, AND BELIEVE IN YOUR OWN UNIVERSE.
Making the initial investment to fund new ideas and companies was exciting, but in a relatively short period of time, Alfred and I had made 27 investments and there was no more money in the fund.
Eventually, Zappos was the only company left in the incubator.
I HAVEN'T SEEN ANY PROSPECTIVE COMPANIES I'D PUT MY MONEY INTO ANY-WAY.
I'M NOT OPTI-MISTIC EITHER.
SO, NOW WHAT?
ZAPPOS IS MAKING SOME REALLY GREAT PROGRESS.
SORRY, TONY.
SEQUOIA STILL ISN'T INTERESTED IN INVESTING IN THEM JUST YET.
I believed with all my heart that Zappos had a great shot at succeeding.
I decided that Zappos was going to be the universe that I wanted to help envision and build. It would be the universe that I believed in.
Investor and Advisor
Entrepreneur

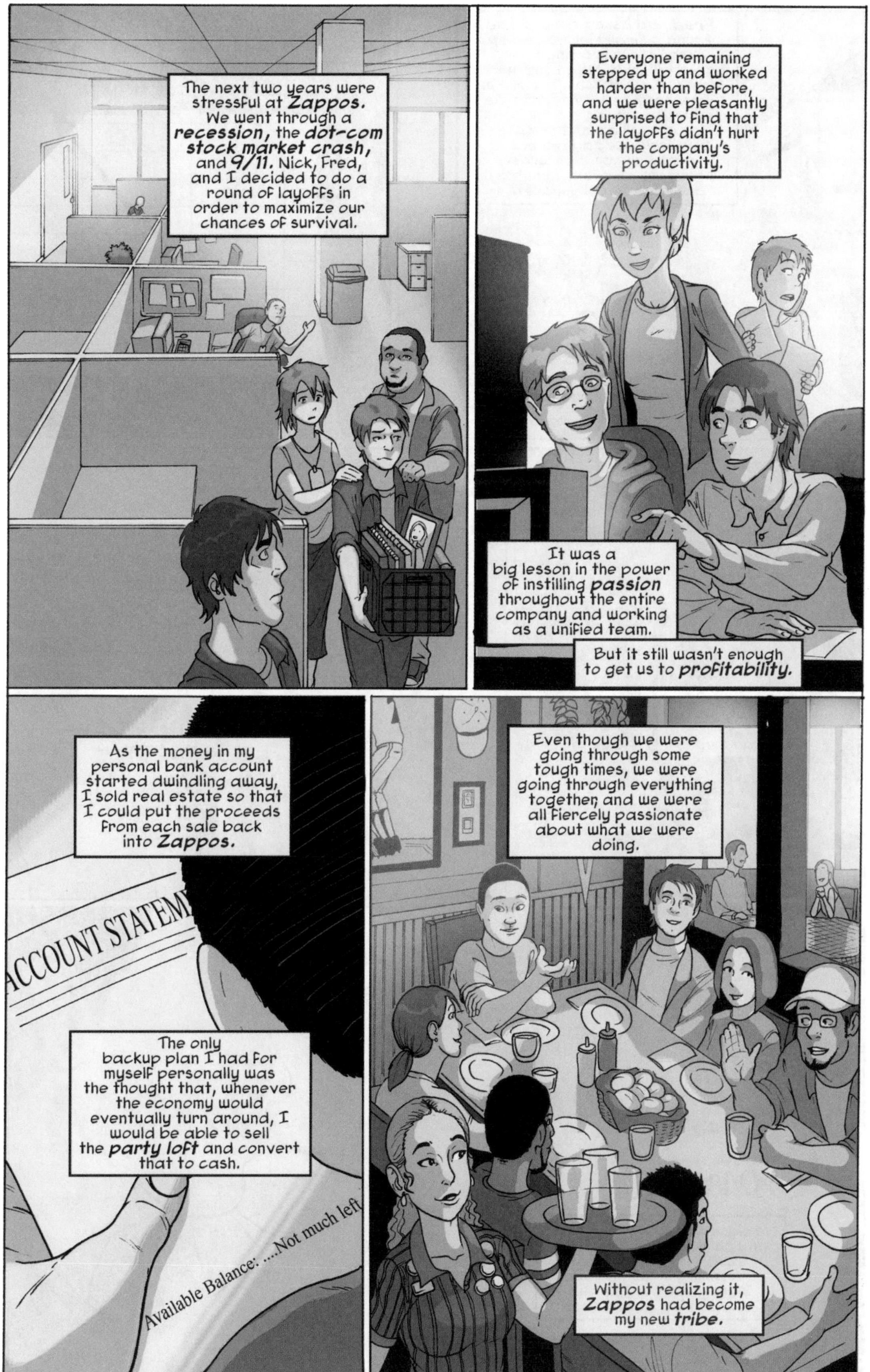
The next two years were stressful at Zappos. We went through a recession, the dot-com stock market crash, and 9/11. Nick, Fred, and I decided to do a round of layoffs in order to maximize our chances of survival.
Everyone remaining stepped up and worked harder than before, and we were pleasantly surprised to find that the layoffs didn't hurt the company's productivity.
It was a big lesson in the power of instilling passion throughout the entire company and working as a unified team.
But it still wasn't enough to get us to profitability.
As the money in my personal bank account started dwindling away, I sold real estate so that I could put the proceeds from each sale back into Zappos.
ACCOUNT STATEM
The only backup plan I had for myself personally was the thought that, whenever the economy would eventually turn around, I would be able to sell the party loft and convert that to cash.
Available Balance: ....Not much left
Even though we were going through some tough times, we were going through everything together, and we were all fiercely passionate about what we were doing.
Without realizing it, Zappos had become my new tribe.

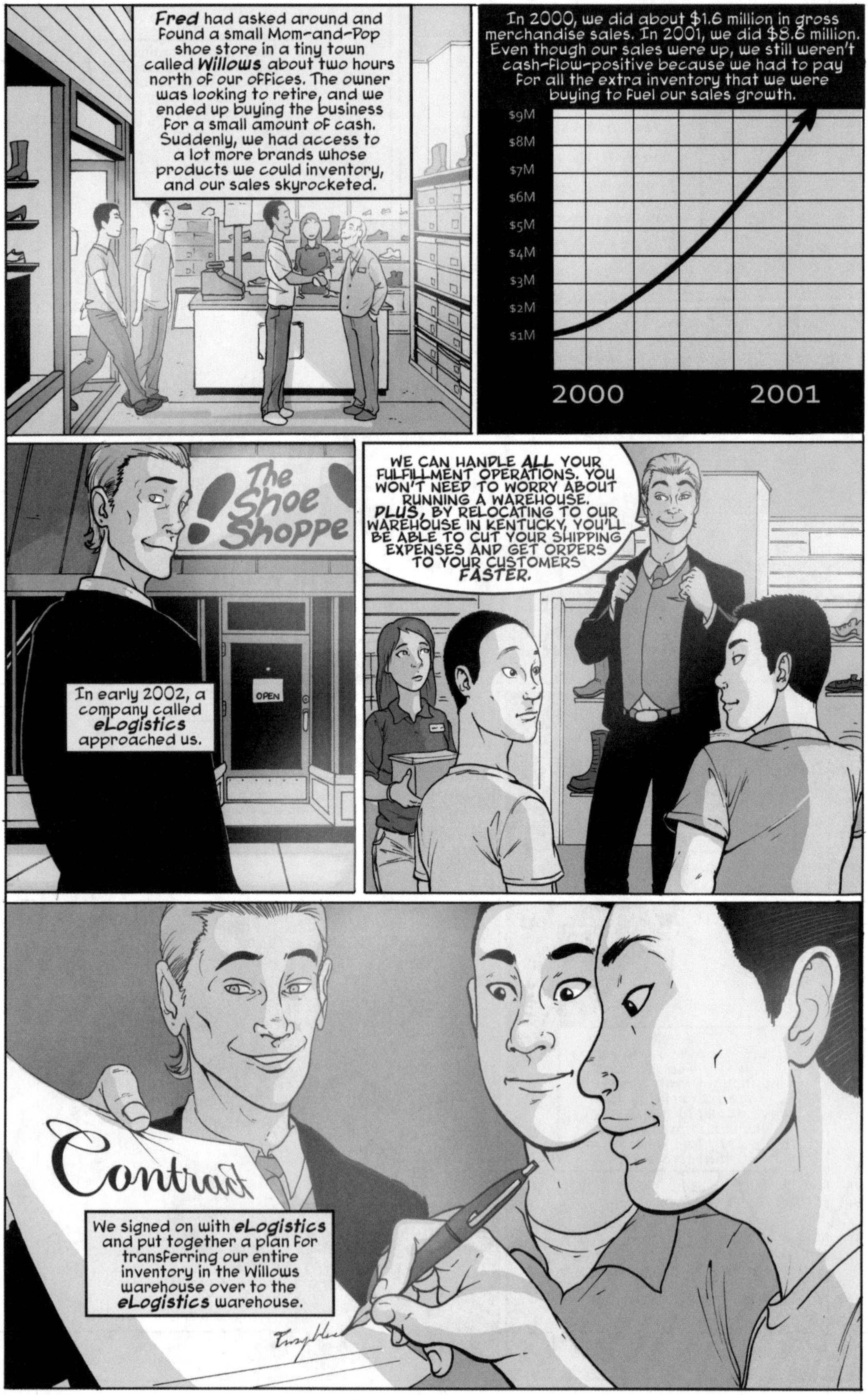
Fred had asked around and found a small Mom-and-Pop shoe store in a tiny town called Willows about two hours north of our offices. The owner was looking to retire, and we ended up buying the business for a small amount of cash. Suddenly, we had access to a lot more brands whose products we could inventory, and our sales skyrocketed.
In 2000, we did about $1.6 million in gross merchandise sales. In 2001, we did $8.6 million. Even though our sales were up, we still weren't cash-flow-positive because we had to pay for all the extra inventory that we were buying to fuel our sales growth.
$9M
$8M
$7M
$6M
$5M
$4M
$3M
$2M
$1M
2000
2001
The Shoe Shoppe
OPEN
In early 2002, a company called eLogistics approached us.
WE CAN HANDLE ALL YOUR FULFILLMENT OPERATIONS. YOU WON'T NEED TO WORRY ABOUT RUNNING A WAREHOUSE. PLUS, BY RELOCATING TO OUR WAREHOUSE IN KENTUCKY, YOU'LL BE ABLE TO CUT YOUR SHIPPING EXPENSES AND GET ORDERS TO YOUR CUSTOMERS FASTER.
Contract
We signed on with eLogistics and put together a plan for transferring our entire inventory in the Willows warehouse over to the eLogistics warehouse.

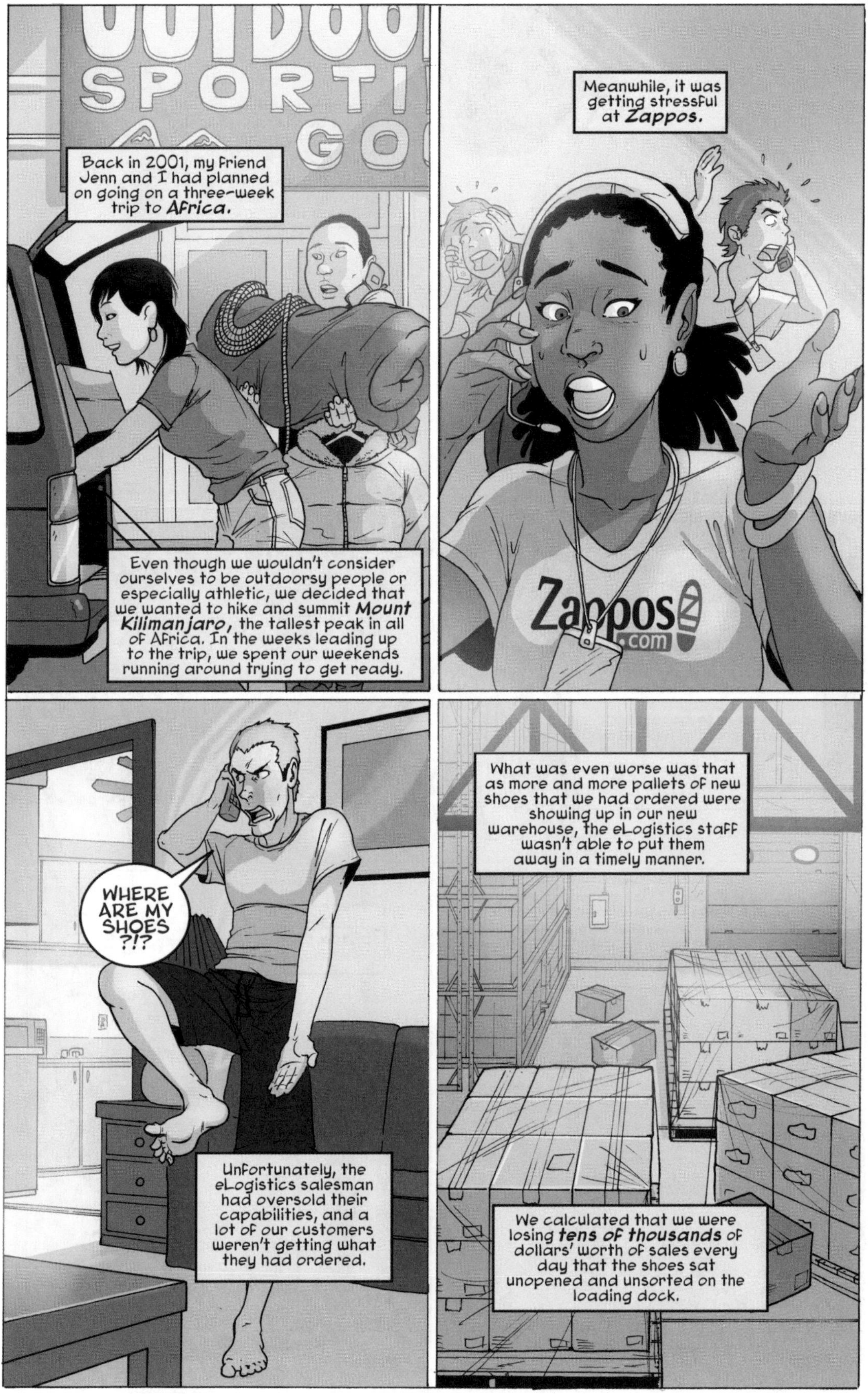
OUTDOOR SPORTING GOODS
Back in 2001, my friend Jenn and I had planned on going on a three-week trip to *Africa.*
Even though we wouldn't consider ourselves to be outdoorsy people or especially athletic, we decided that we wanted to hike and summit *Mount Kilimanjaro,* the tallest peak in all of Africa. In the weeks leading up to the trip, we spent our weekends running around trying to get ready.
Meanwhile, it was getting stressful at *Zappos.*
Zappos.com
WHERE ARE MY SHOES ?!?
Unfortunately, the eLogistics salesman had oversold their capabilities, and a lot of our customers weren't getting what they had ordered.
What was even worse was that as more and more pallets of new shoes that we had ordered were showing up in our new warehouse, the eLogistics staff wasn't able to put them away in a timely manner.
We calculated that we were losing ***tens of thousands*** of dollars' worth of sales every day that the shoes sat unopened and unsorted on the loading dock.

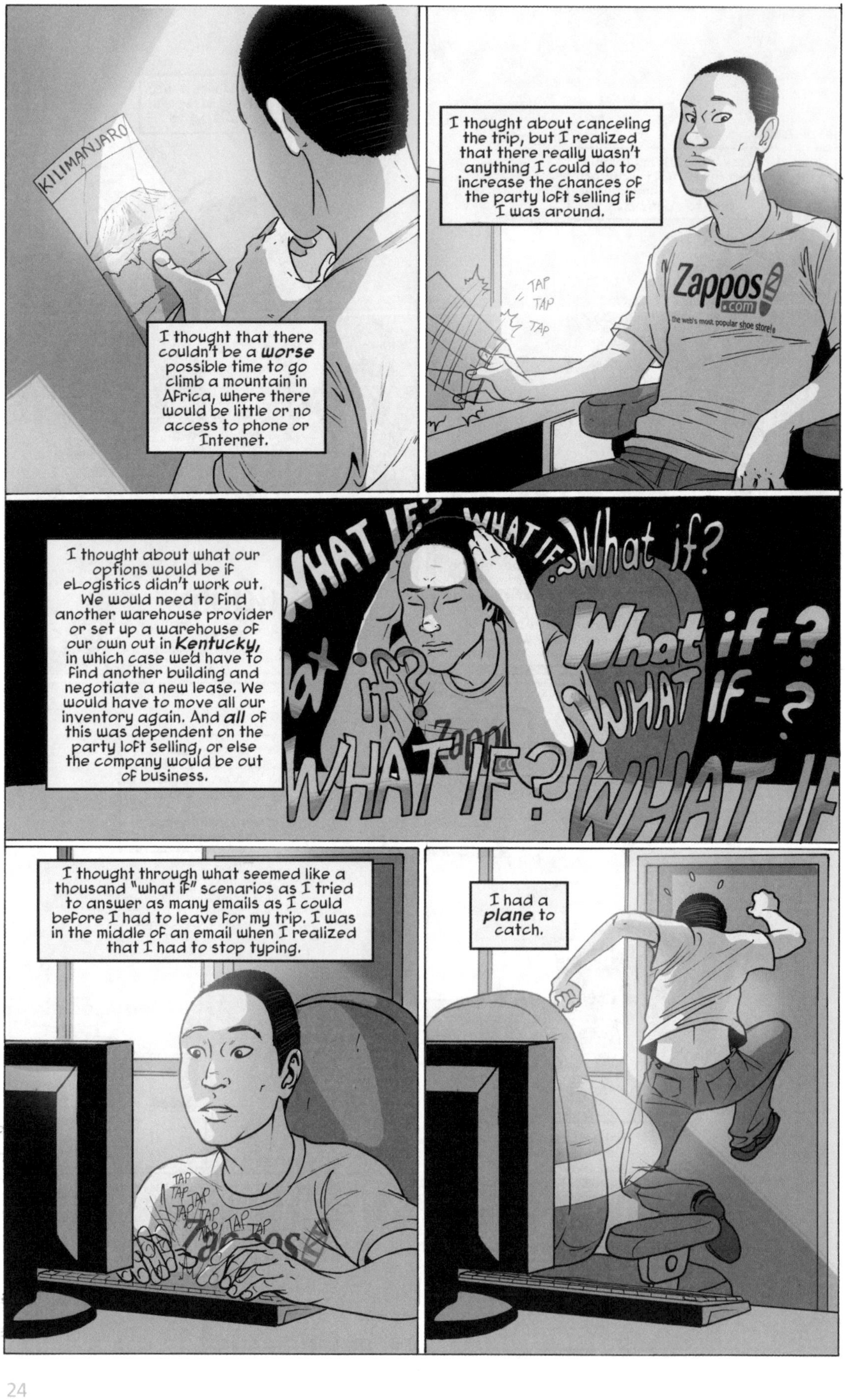
KILIMANJARO
I thought that there couldn't be a ***worse*** possible time to go climb a mountain in Africa, where there would be little or no access to phone or Internet.
I thought about canceling the trip, but I realized that there really wasn't anything I could do to increase the chances of the party loft selling if I was around.
TAP TAP TAP
Zappos.com
the web's most popular shoe store!
I thought about what our options would be if eLogistics didn't work out. We would need to find another warehouse provider or set up a warehouse of our own out in ***Kentucky,*** in which case we'd have to find another building and negotiate a new lease. We would have to move all our inventory again. And ***all*** of this was dependent on the party loft selling, or else the company would be out of business.
What if?
What if -?
WHAT IF -?
WHAT IF?
I thought through what seemed like a thousand "what if" scenarios as I tried to answer as many emails as I could before I had to leave for my trip. I was in the middle of an email when I realized that I had to stop typing.
TAP TAP TAP TAP TAP TAP TAP TAP
I had a ***plane*** to catch.

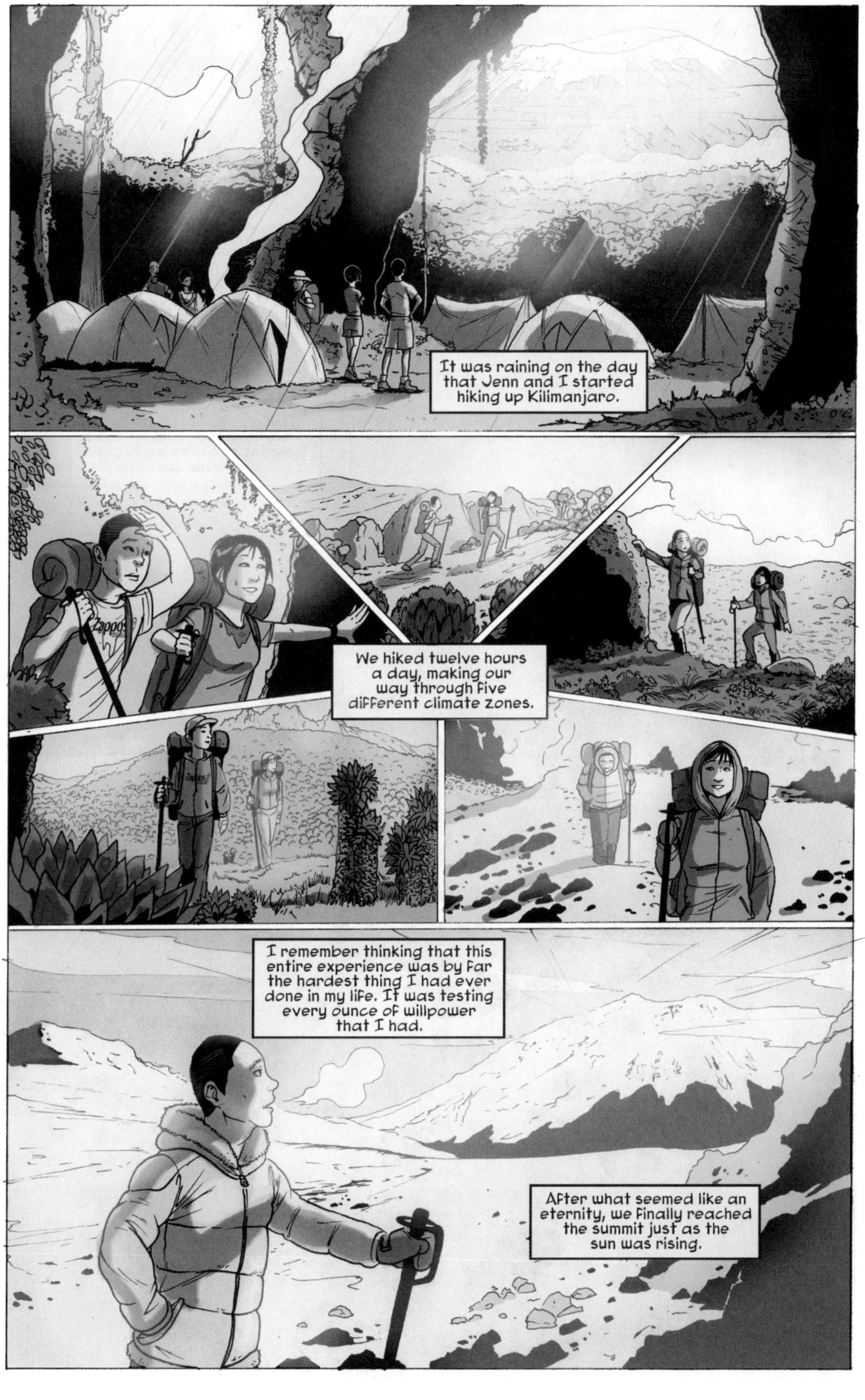
It was raining on the day that Jenn and I started hiking up Kilimanjaro.
We hiked twelve hours a day, making our way through five different climate zones.
I remember thinking that this entire experience was by far the hardest thing I had ever done in my life. It was testing every ounce of willpower that I had.
After what seemed like an eternity, we finally reached the summit just as the sun was rising.

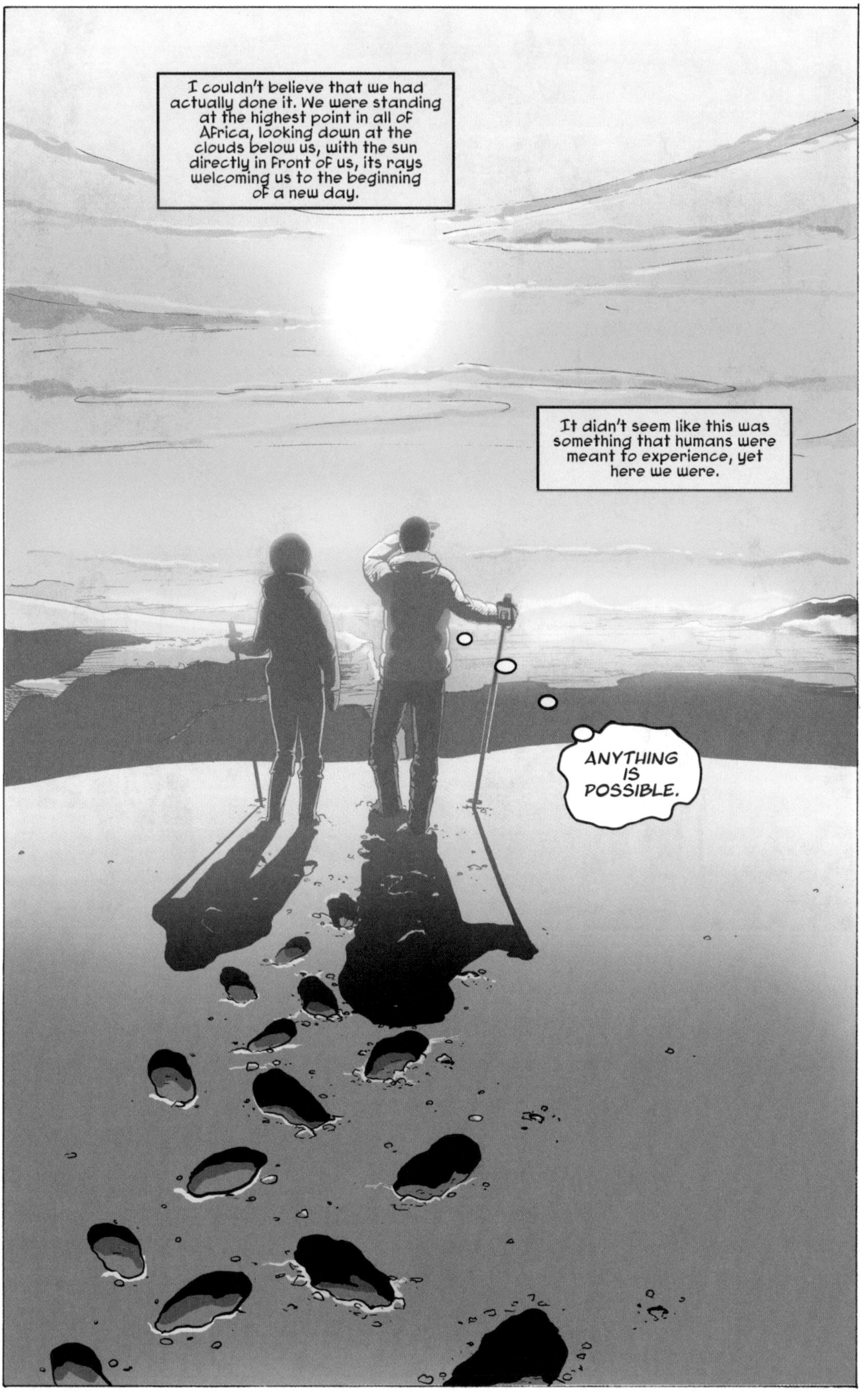
I couldn't believe that we had actually done it. We were standing at the highest point in all of Africa, looking down at the clouds below us, with the sun directly in front of us, its rays welcoming us to the beginning of a new day.
It didn't seem like this was something that humans were meant to experience, yet here we were.
ANYTHING IS POSSIBLE.

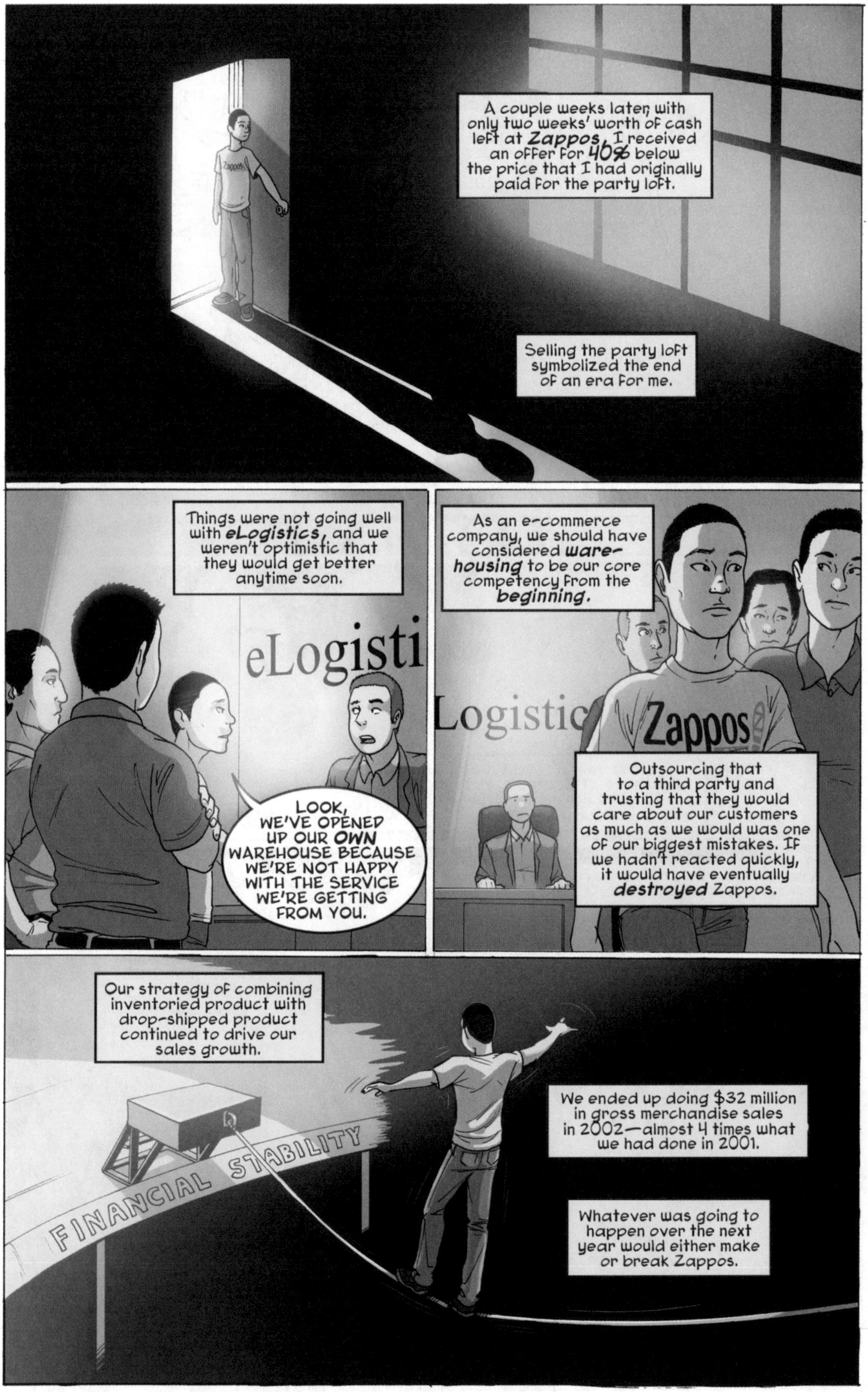
A couple weeks later, with only two weeks' worth of cash left at Zappos, I received an offer for 40% below the price that I had originally paid for the party loft.
Selling the party loft symbolized the end of an era for me.
Things were not going well with eLogistics, and we weren't optimistic that they would get better anytime soon.
eLogisti
LOOK, WE'VE OPENED UP OUR OWN WAREHOUSE BECAUSE WE'RE NOT HAPPY WITH THE SERVICE WE'RE GETTING FROM YOU.
As an e-commerce company, we should have considered warehousing to be our core competency from the beginning.
Logistic
Zappos
Outsourcing that to a third party and trusting that they would care about our customers as much as we would was one of our biggest mistakes. If we hadn't reacted quickly, it would have eventually destroyed Zappos.
Our strategy of combining inventoried product with drop-shipped product continued to drive our sales growth.
FINANCIAL STABILITY
We ended up doing $32 million in gross merchandise sales in 2002—almost 4 times what we had done in 2001.
Whatever was going to happen over the next year would either make or break Zappos.

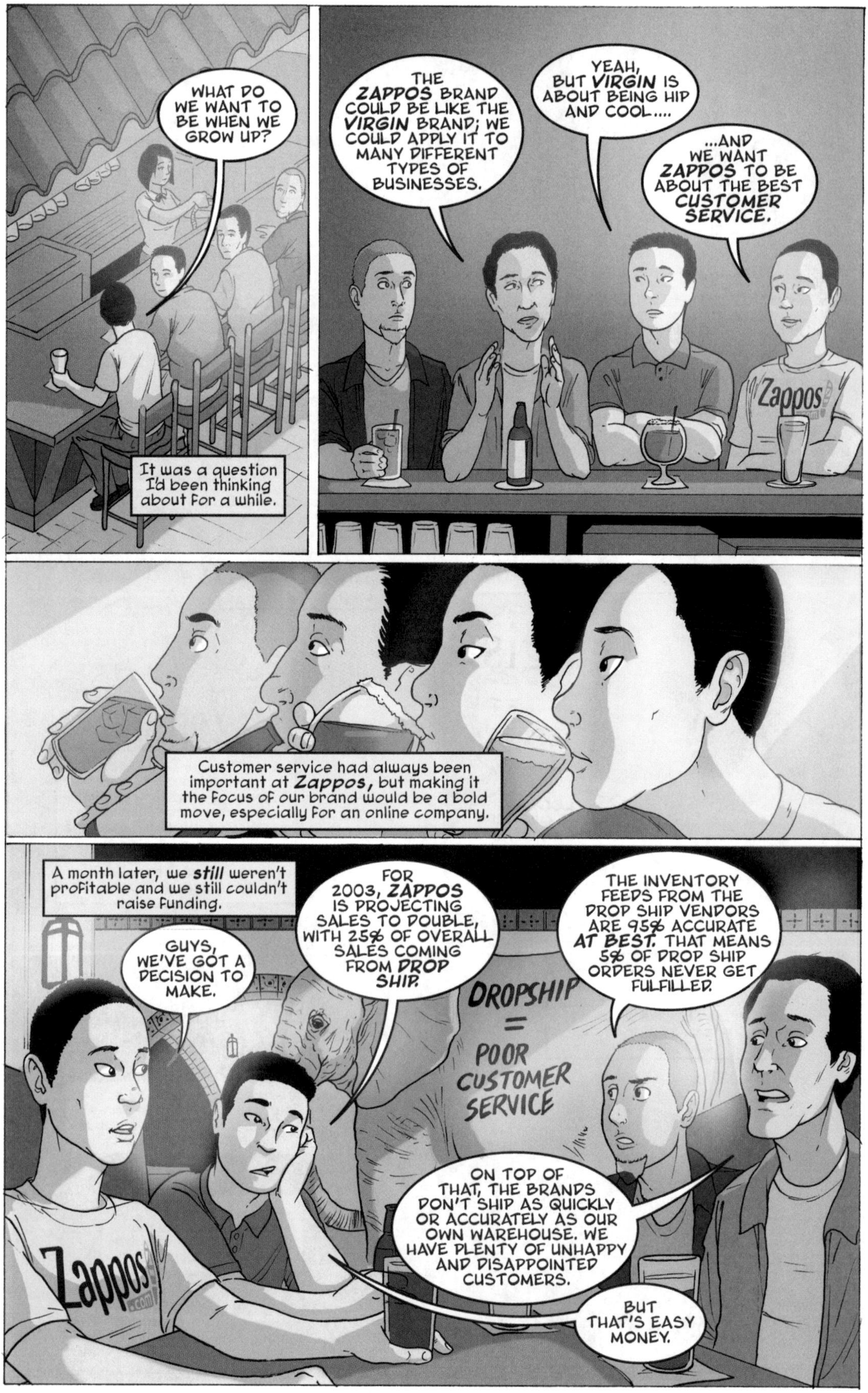

WHAT DO WE WANT TO BE WHEN WE GROW UP?
It was a question I'd been thinking about for a while.
THE ZAPPOS BRAND COULD BE LIKE THE VIRGIN BRAND; WE COULD APPLY IT TO MANY DIFFERENT TYPES OF BUSINESSES.
YEAH, BUT VIRGIN IS ABOUT BEING HIP AND COOL....
...AND WE WANT ZAPPOS TO BE ABOUT THE BEST CUSTOMER SERVICE.
Zappos
Customer service had always been important at Zappos, but making it the focus of our brand would be a bold move, especially for an online company.
A month later, we still weren't profitable and we still couldn't raise funding.
GUYS, WE'VE GOT A DECISION TO MAKE.
FOR 2003, ZAPPOS IS PROJECTING SALES TO DOUBLE, WITH 25% OF OVERALL SALES COMING FROM DROP SHIP.
THE INVENTORY FEEDS FROM THE DROP SHIP VENDORS ARE 95% ACCURATE AT BEST. THAT MEANS 5% OF DROP SHIP ORDERS NEVER GET FULFILLED.
DROPSHIP = POOR CUSTOMER SERVICE
ON TOP OF THAT, THE BRANDS DON'T SHIP AS QUICKLY OR ACCURATELY AS OUR OWN WAREHOUSE. WE HAVE PLENTY OF UNHAPPY AND DISAPPOINTED CUSTOMERS.
BUT THAT'S EASY MONEY.
Zappos .com

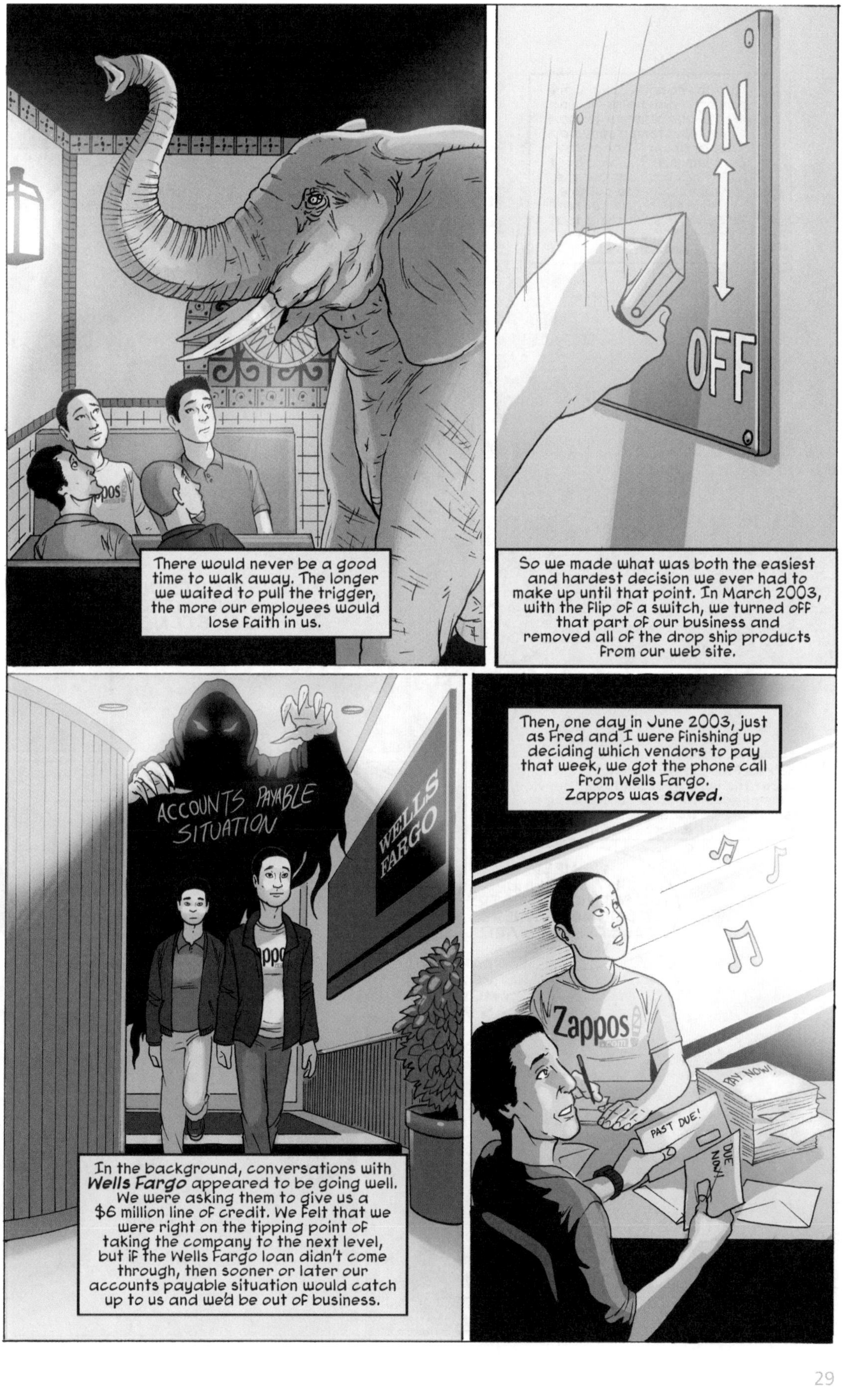
There would never be a good time to walk away. The longer we waited to pull the trigger, the more our employees would lose faith in us.
ON
OFF
So we made what was both the easiest and hardest decision we ever had to make up until that point. In March 2003, with the flip of a switch, we turned off that part of our business and removed all of the drop ship products from our web site.
ACCOUNTS PAYABLE SITUATION
WELLS FARGO
In the background, conversations with **Wells Fargo** appeared to be going well. We were asking them to give us a $6 million line of credit. We felt that we were right on the tipping point of taking the company to the next level, but if the Wells Fargo loan didn't come through, then sooner or later our accounts payable situation would catch up to us and we'd be out of business.
Then, one day in June 2003, just as Fred and I were finishing up deciding which vendors to pay that week, we got the phone call from Wells Fargo.
Zappos was ***saved.***
Zappos
PAY NOW!
PAST DUE!
DUE NOW!

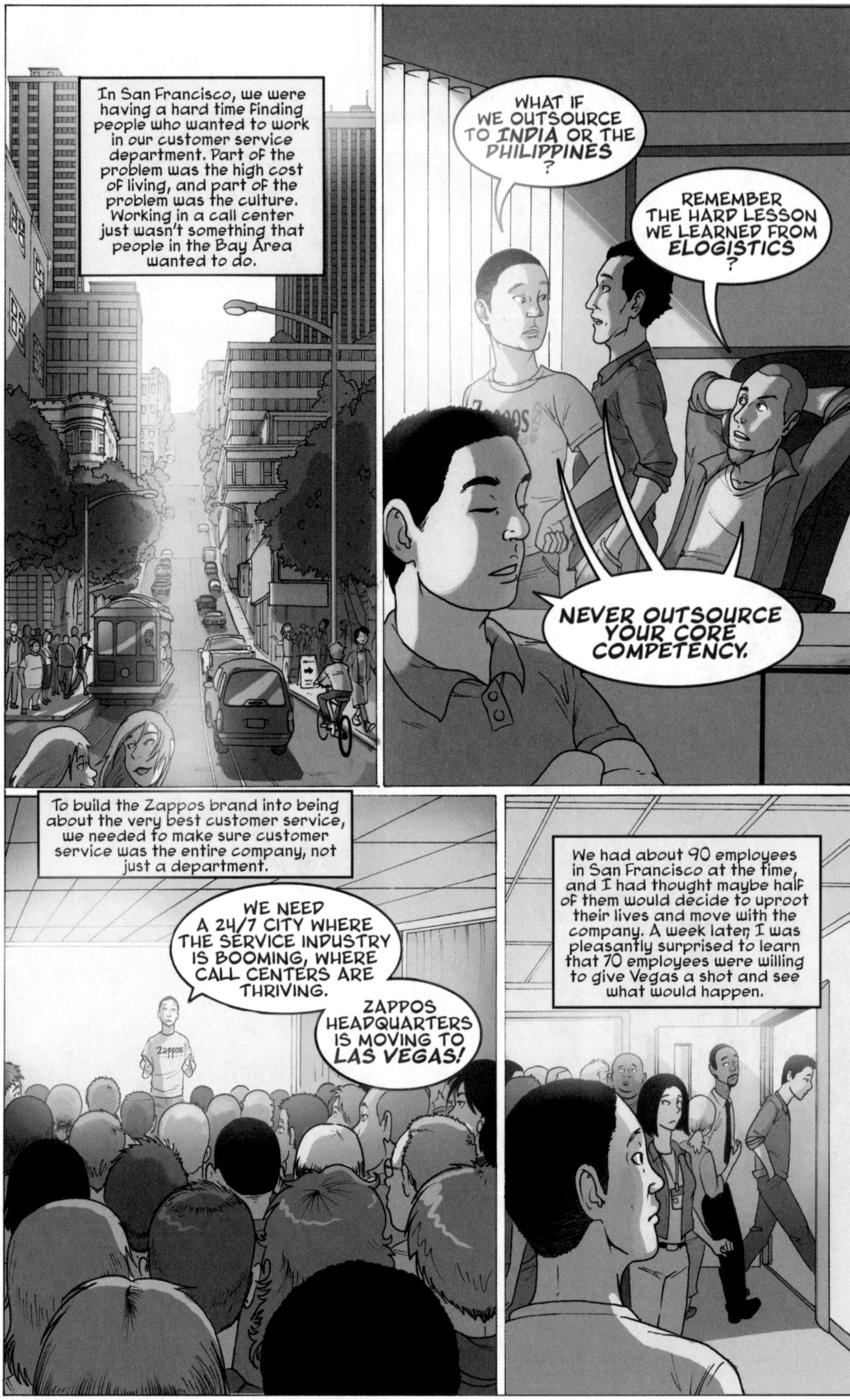
In San Francisco, we were having a hard time finding people who wanted to work in our customer service department. Part of the problem was the high cost of living, and part of the problem was the culture. Working in a call center just wasn't something that people in the Bay Area wanted to do.
WHAT IF WE OUTSOURCE TO INDIA OR THE PHILIPPINES?
REMEMBER THE HARD LESSON WE LEARNED FROM ELOGISTICS?
NEVER OUTSOURCE YOUR CORE COMPETENCY.
To build the Zappos brand into being about the very best customer service, we needed to make sure customer service was the entire company, not just a department.
WE NEED A 24/7 CITY WHERE THE SERVICE INDUSTRY IS BOOMING, WHERE CALL CENTERS ARE THRIVING.
ZAPPOS HEADQUARTERS IS MOVING TO LAS VEGAS!
We had about 90 employees in San Francisco at the time, and I had thought maybe half of them would decide to uproot their lives and move with the company. A week later, I was pleasantly surprised to learn that 70 employees were willing to give Vegas a shot and see what would happen.

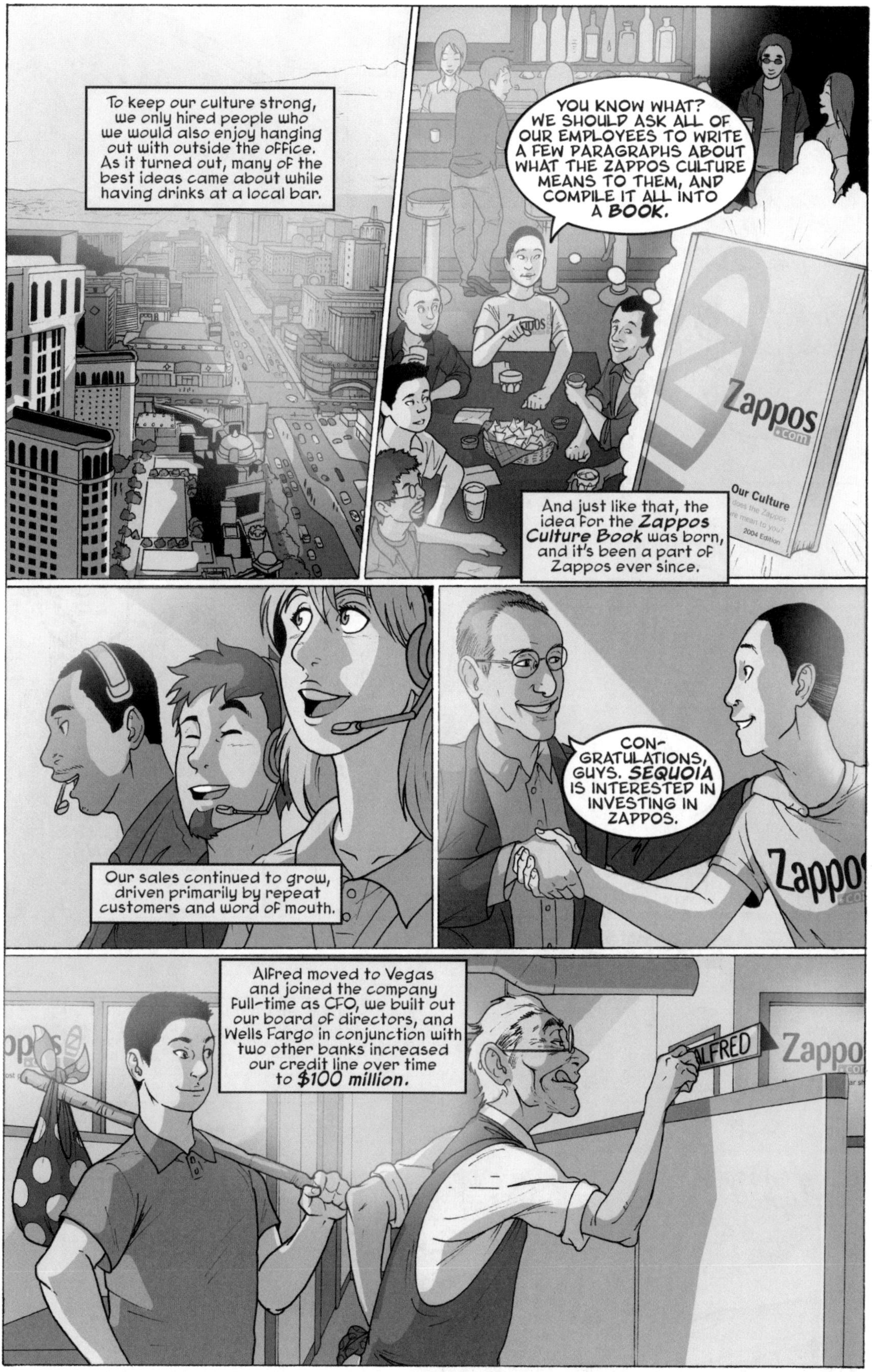
To keep our culture strong, we only hired people who we would also enjoy hanging out with outside the office. As it turned out, many of the best ideas came about while having drinks at a local bar.
YOU KNOW WHAT? WE SHOULD ASK ALL OF OUR EMPLOYEES TO WRITE A FEW PARAGRAPHS ABOUT WHAT THE ZAPPOS CULTURE MEANS TO THEM, AND COMPILE IT ALL INTO A BOOK.
Zappos .com
Our Culture
2004 Edition
And just like that, the idea for the Zappos Culture Book was born, and it's been a part of Zappos ever since.
Our sales continued to grow, driven primarily by repeat customers and word of mouth.
CON-GRATULATIONS, GUYS. SEQUOIA IS INTERESTED IN INVESTING IN ZAPPOS.
Zappos
Alfred moved to Vegas and joined the company full-time as CFO, we built out our board of directors, and Wells Fargo in conjunction with two other banks increased our credit line over time to $100 million.
ALFRED
Zappos

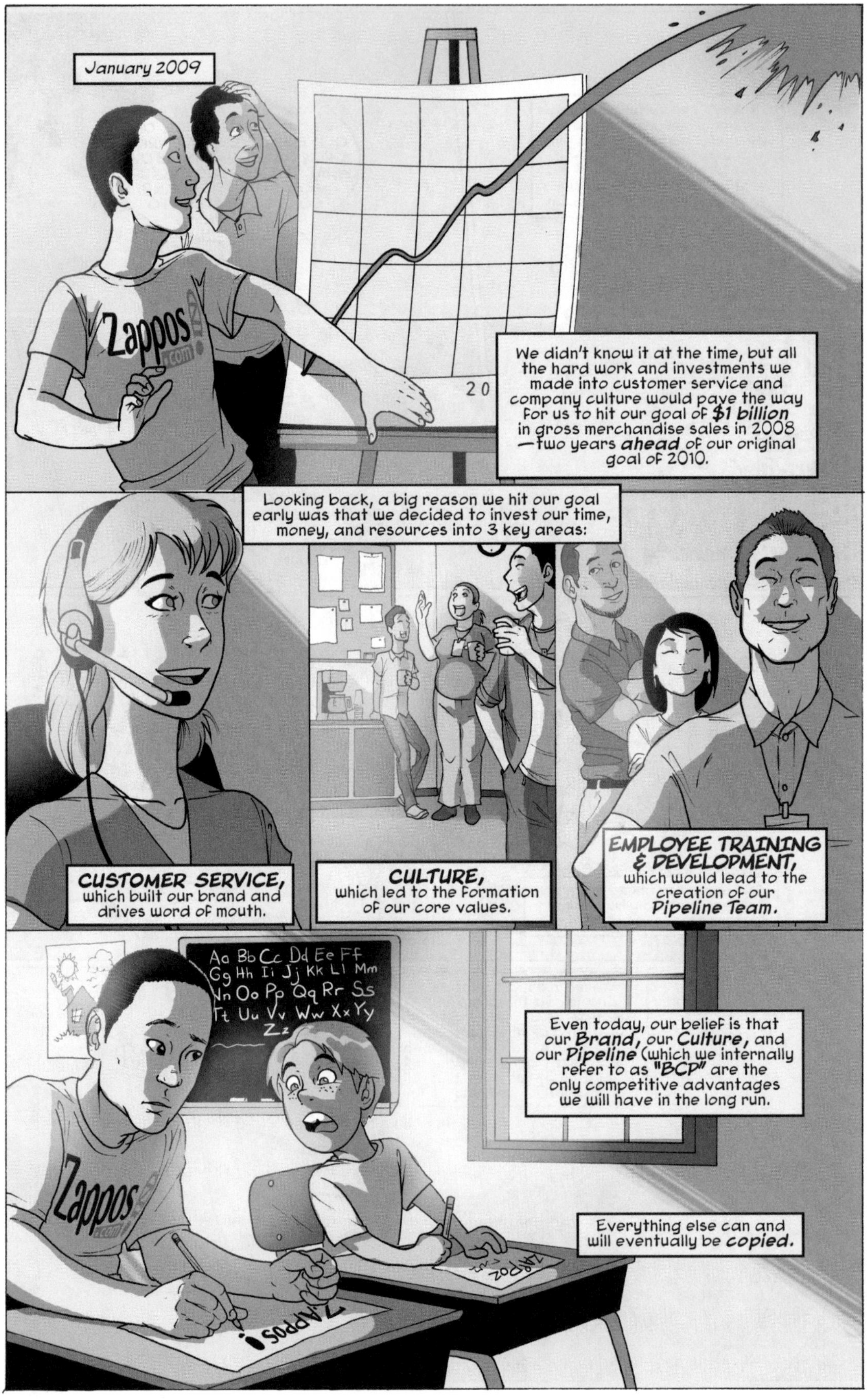
January 2009
20
We didn't know it at the time, but all the hard work and investments we made into customer service and company culture would pave the way for us to hit our goal of $1 billion in gross merchandise sales in 2008 —two years ahead of our original goal of 2010.
Looking back, a big reason we hit our goal early was that we decided to invest our time, money, and resources into 3 key areas:
CUSTOMER SERVICE, which built our brand and drives word of mouth.
CULTURE, which led to the formation of our core values.
EMPLOYEE TRAINING & DEVELOPMENT, which would lead to the creation of our Pipeline Team.
Aa Bb Cc Dd Ee Ff Gg Hh Ii Jj Kk Ll Mm Nn Oo Pp Qq Rr Ss Tt Uu Vv Ww Xx Yy Zz
Even today, our belief is that our Brand, our Culture, and our Pipeline (which we internally refer to as "BCP" are the only competitive advantages we will have in the long run.
Everything else can and will eventually be copied.

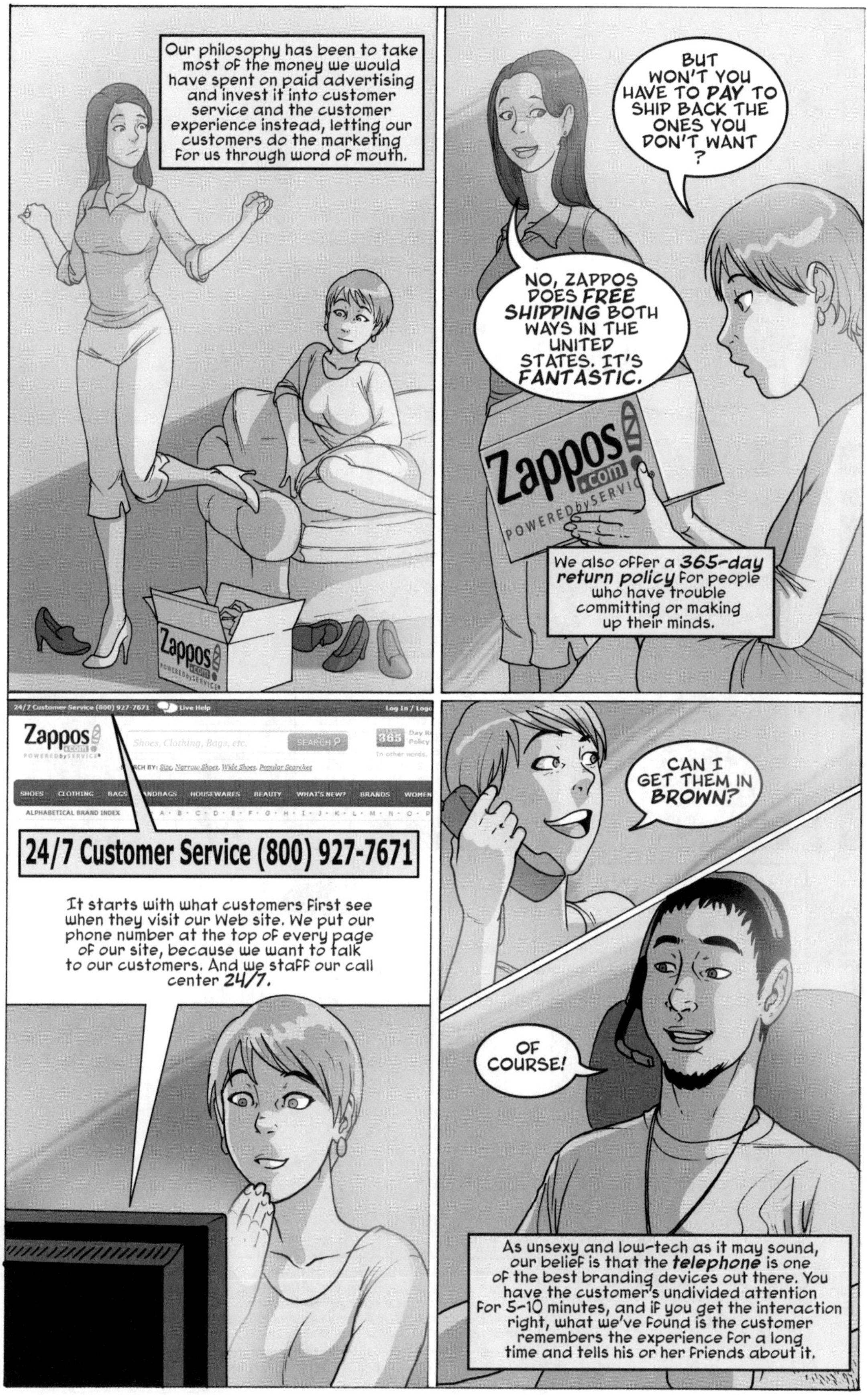
Our philosophy has been to take most of the money we would have spent on paid advertising and invest it into customer service and the customer experience instead, letting our customers do the marketing for us through word of mouth.
Zappos .com POWERED by SERVICE
BUT WON'T YOU HAVE TO PAY TO SHIP BACK THE ONES YOU DON'T WANT ?
NO, ZAPPOS DOES FREE SHIPPING BOTH WAYS IN THE UNITED STATES. IT'S FANTASTIC.
Zappos .com POWERED by SERVIC
We also offer a 365-day return policy for people who have trouble committing or making up their minds.
24/7 Customer Service (800) 927-7671
Live Help
Zappos .com POWERED by SERVICE
SEARCH
365
SHOES
CLOTHING
HOUSEWARES
BEAUTY
WHAT'S NEW?
BRANDS
ALPHABETICAL BRAND INDEX
24/7 Customer Service (800) 927-7671
It starts with what customers first see when they visit our Web site. We put our phone number at the top of every page of our site, because we want to talk to our customers. And we staff our call center 24/7.
CAN I GET THEM IN BROWN?
OF COURSE!
As unsexy and low-tech as it may sound, our belief is that the telephone is one of the best branding devices out there. You have the customer's undivided attention for 5-10 minutes, and if you get the interaction right, what we've found is the customer remembers the experience for a long time and tells his or her friends about it.

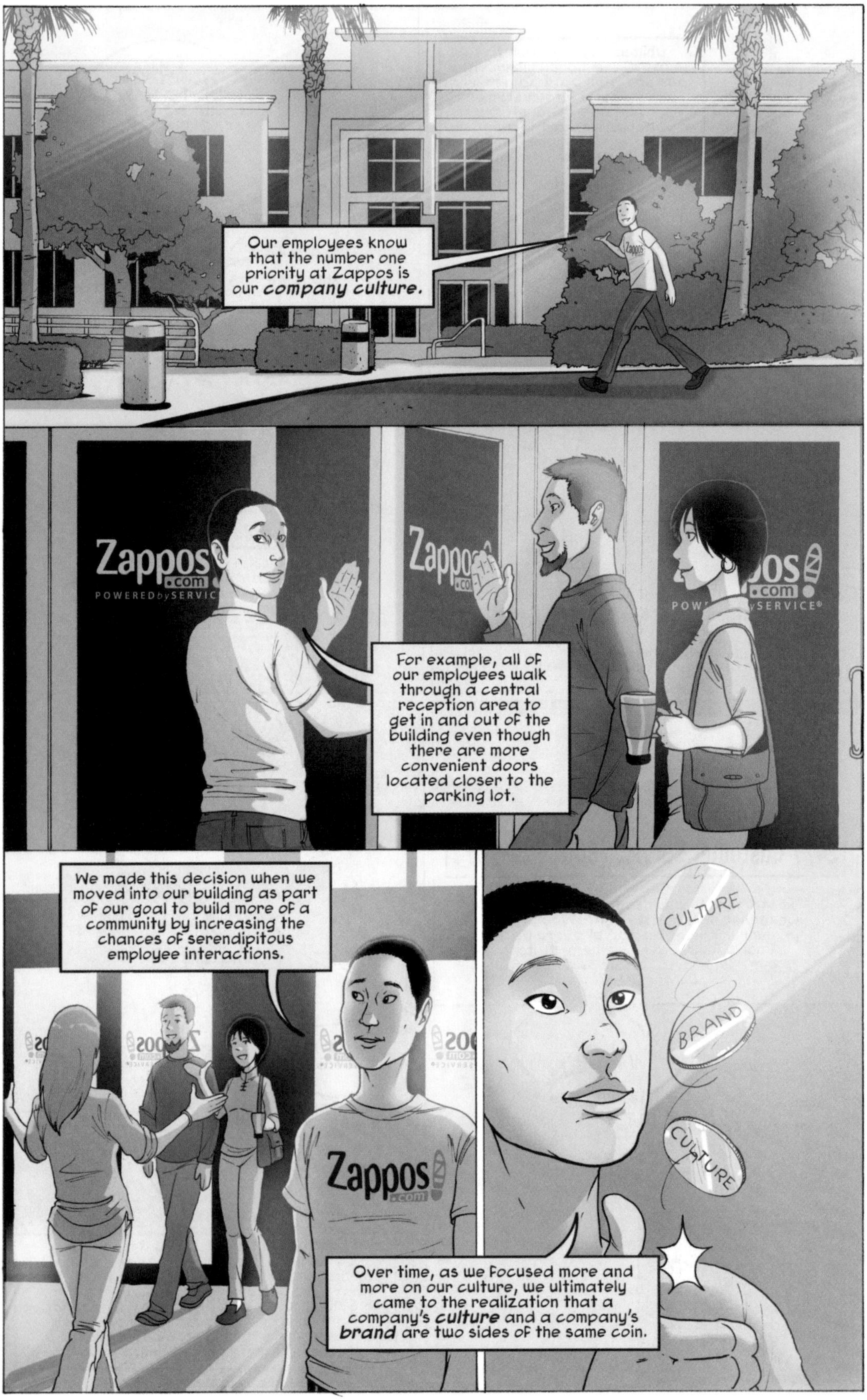
Our employees know that the number one priority at Zappos is our *company culture.*
For example, all of our employees walk through a central reception area to get in and out of the building even though there are more convenient doors located closer to the parking lot.
We made this decision when we moved into our building as part of our goal to build more of a community by increasing the chances of serendipitous employee interactions.
CULTURE
BRAND
CULTURE
Over time, as we focused more and more on our culture, we ultimately came to the realization that a company's **culture** and a company's **brand** are two sides of the same coin.

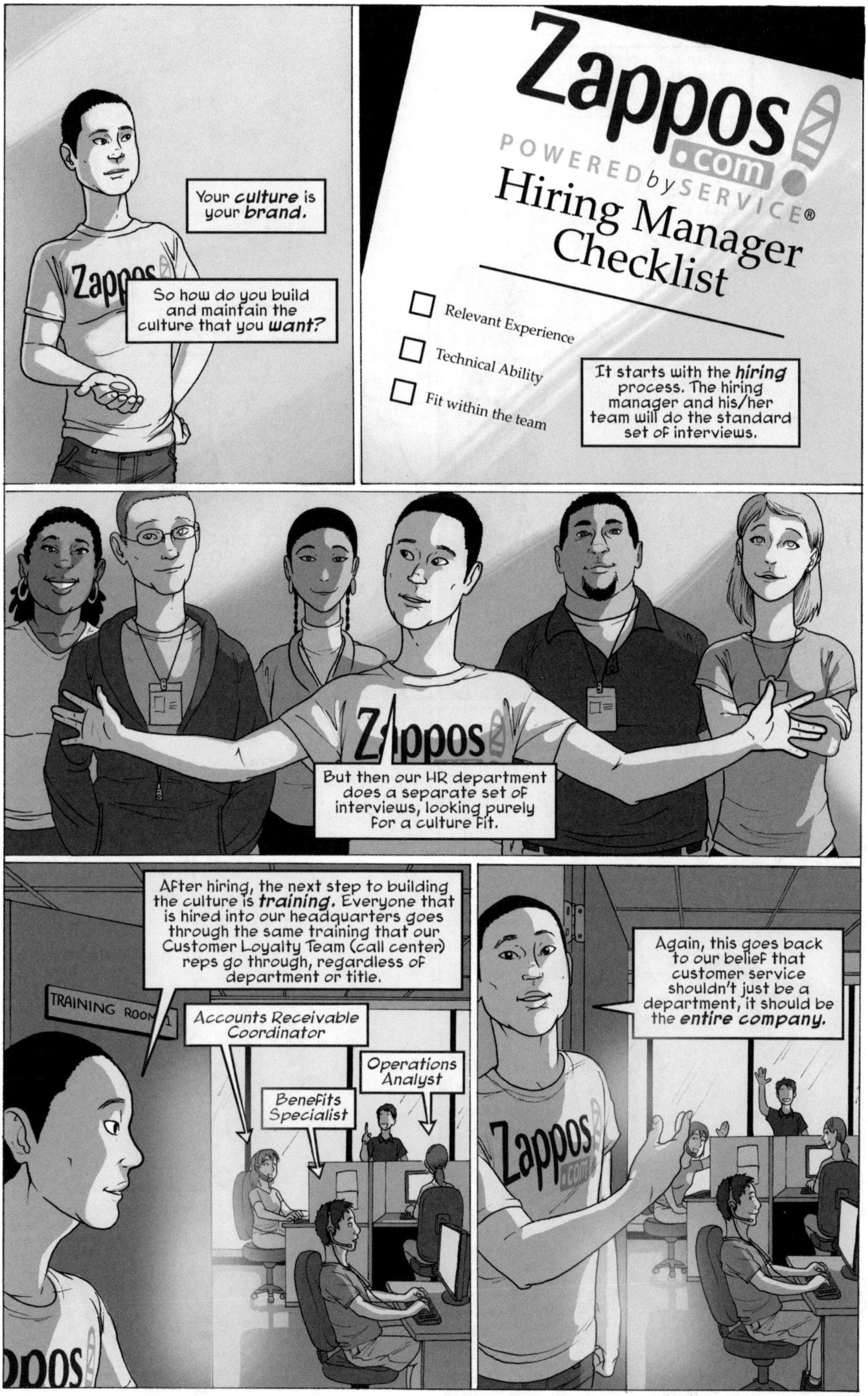
Your culture is your brand.
So how do you build and maintain the culture that you want?
Zappos .com
POWERED by SERVICE®
Hiring Manager Checklist
Relevant Experience
Technical Ability
Fit within the team
It starts with the hiring process. The hiring manager and his/her team will do the standard set of interviews.
But then our HR department does a separate set of interviews, looking purely for a culture fit.
After hiring, the next step to building the culture is training. Everyone that is hired into our headquarters goes through the same training that our Customer Loyalty Team (call center) reps go through, regardless of department or title.
TRAINING
Accounts Receivable Coordinator
Operations Analyst
Benefits Specialist
Again, this goes back to our belief that customer service shouldn't just be a department, it should be the entire company.

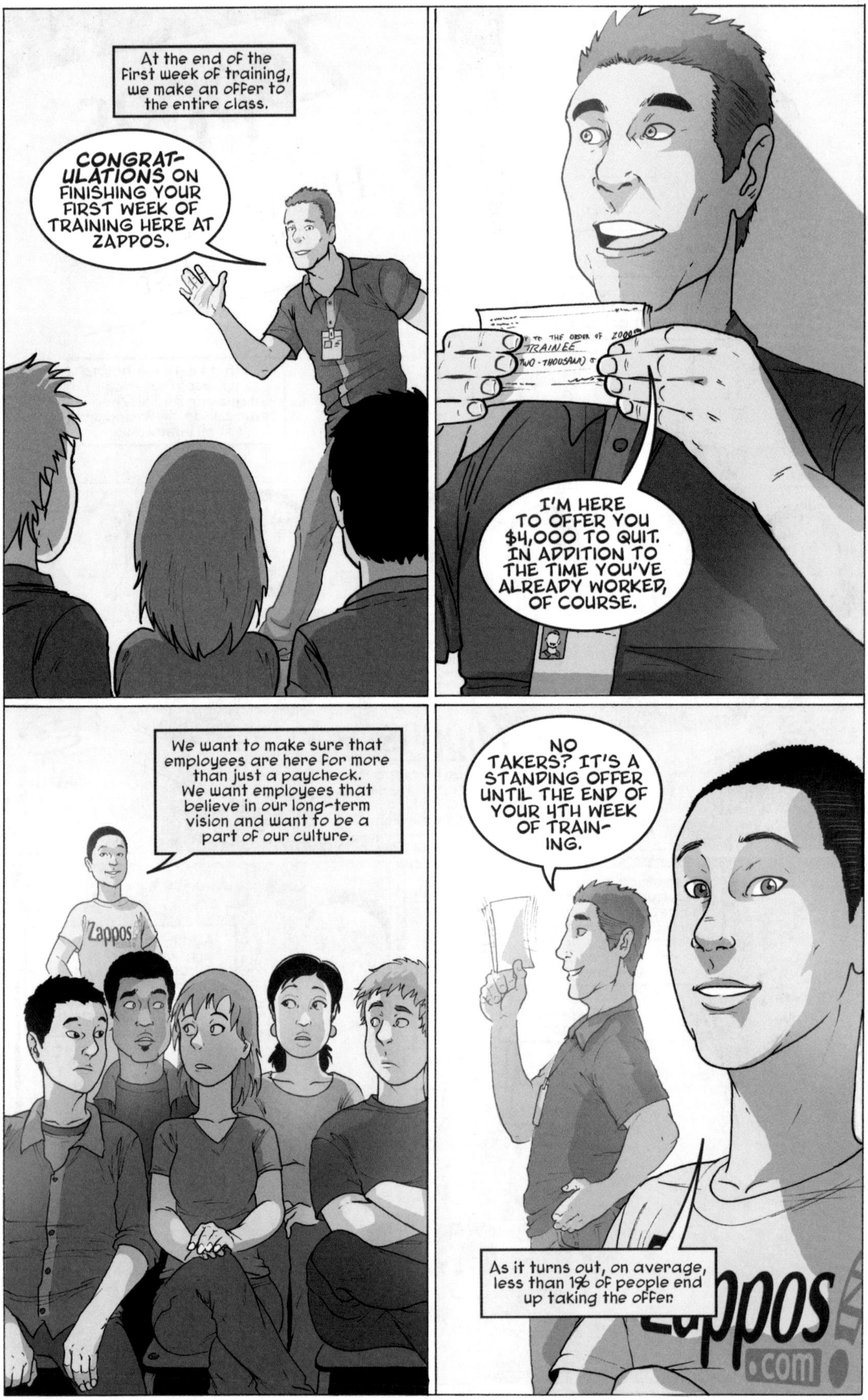
At the end of the first week of training, we make an offer to the entire class.
CONGRATULATIONS ON FINISHING YOUR FIRST WEEK OF TRAINING HERE AT ZAPPOS.
I'M HERE TO OFFER YOU $4,000 TO QUIT. IN ADDITION TO THE TIME YOU'VE ALREADY WORKED, OF COURSE.
We want to make sure that employees are here for more than just a paycheck. We want employees that believe in our long-term vision and want to be a part of our culture.
NO TAKERS? IT'S A STANDING OFFER UNTIL THE END OF YOUR 4TH WEEK OF TRAINING.
As it turns out, on average, less than 1% of people end up taking the offer.

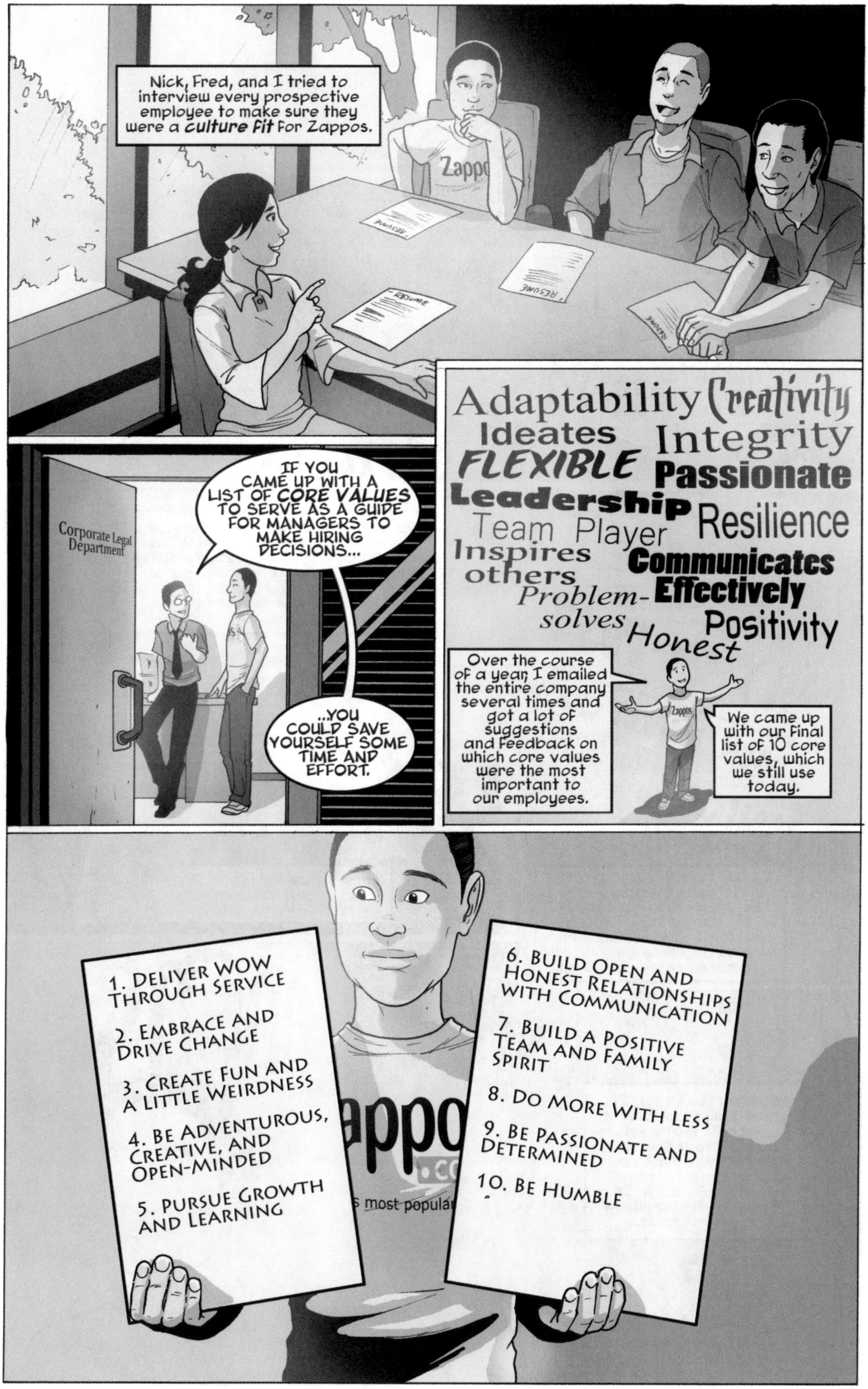
Nick, Fred, and I tried to interview every prospective employee to make sure they were a culture fit for Zappos.
IF YOU CAME UP WITH A LIST OF CORE VALUES TO SERVE AS A GUIDE FOR MANAGERS TO MAKE HIRING DECISIONS...
...YOU COULD SAVE YOURSELF SOME TIME AND EFFORT.
Corporate Legal Department
Adaptability Creativity Ideates Integrity FLEXIBLE Passionate Leadership Resilience Team Player Inspires others Communicates Effectively Problem-solves Positivity Honest
Over the course of a year, I emailed the entire company several times and got a lot of suggestions and feedback on which core values were the most important to our employees.
We came up with our final list of 10 core values, which we still use today.
1. Deliver WOW Through Service
2. Embrace and Drive Change
3. Create Fun and a Little Weirdness
4. Be Adventurous, Creative, and Open-Minded
5. Pursue Growth and Learning
6. Build Open and Honest Relationships with Communication
7. Build a Positive Team and Family Spirit
8. Do More With Less
9. Be Passionate and Determined
10. Be Humble

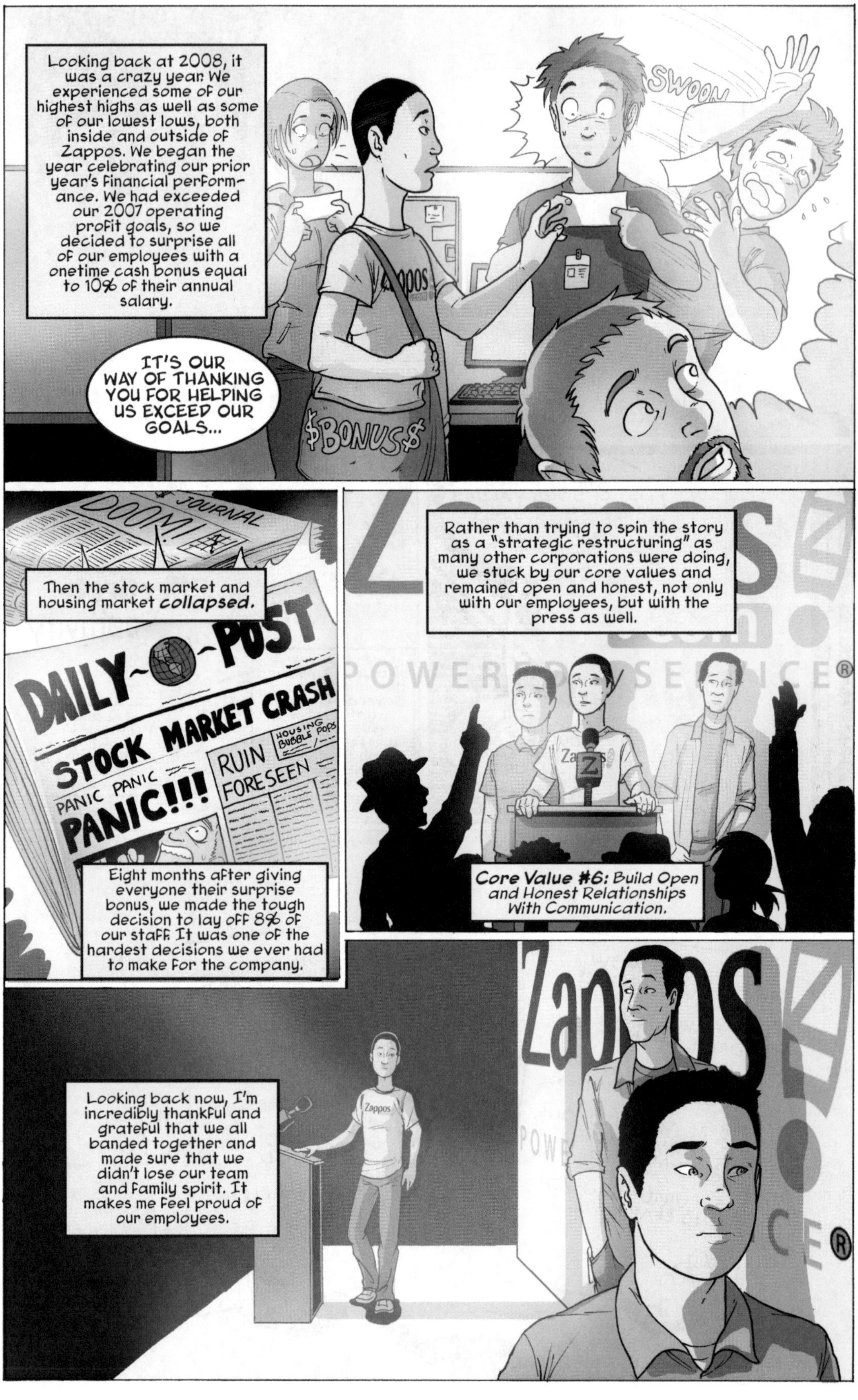
Looking back at 2008, it was a crazy year. We experienced some of our highest highs as well as some of our lowest lows, both inside and outside of Zappos. We began the year celebrating our prior year's financial performance. We had exceeded our 2007 operating profit goals, so we decided to surprise all of our employees with a onetime cash bonus equal to 10% of their annual salary.
SWOON
IT'S OUR WAY OF THANKING YOU FOR HELPING US EXCEED OUR GOALS...
$BONUS$
JOURNAL
DOOM!
Then the stock market and housing market *collapsed.*
DAILY-POST
STOCK MARKET CRASH
HOUSING BUBBLE POPS
STOCK
PANIC PANIC
PANIC!!!
RUIN FORESEEN
Eight months after giving everyone their surprise bonus, we made the tough decision to lay off 8% of our staff. It was one of the hardest decisions we ever had to make for the company.
Rather than trying to spin the story as a "strategic restructuring" as many other corporations were doing, we stuck by our core values and remained open and honest, not only with our employees, but with the press as well.
POWERED BY SERVICE®
Core Value #6: *Build Open and Honest Relationships With Communication.*
Looking back now, I'm incredibly thankful and grateful that we all banded together and made sure that we didn't lose our team and family spirit. It makes me feel proud of our employees.

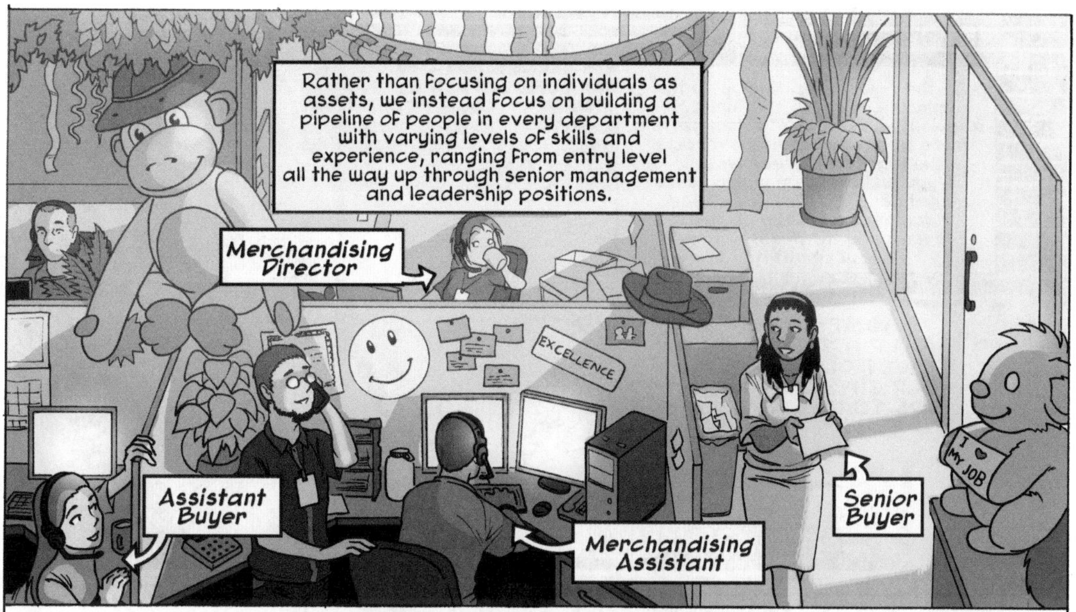
Rather than focusing on individuals as assets, we instead focus on building a pipeline of people in every department with varying levels of skills and experience, ranging from entry level all the way up through senior management and leadership positions.
Merchandising Director
EXCELLENCE
Assistant Buyer
Merchandising Assistant
Senior Buyer
I ♥ MY JOB

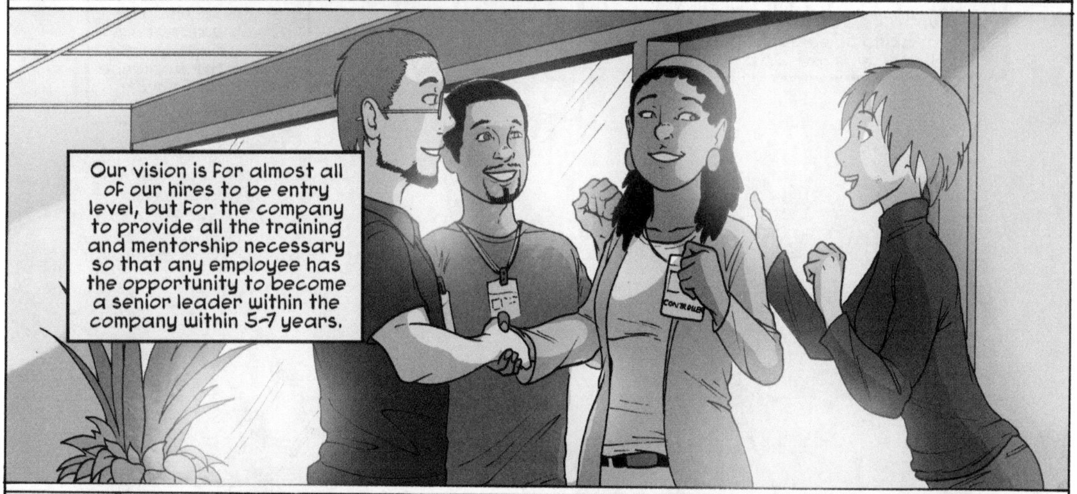
Our vision is for almost all of our hires to be entry level, but for the company to provide all the training and mentorship necessary so that any employee has the opportunity to become a senior leader within the company within 5-7 years.

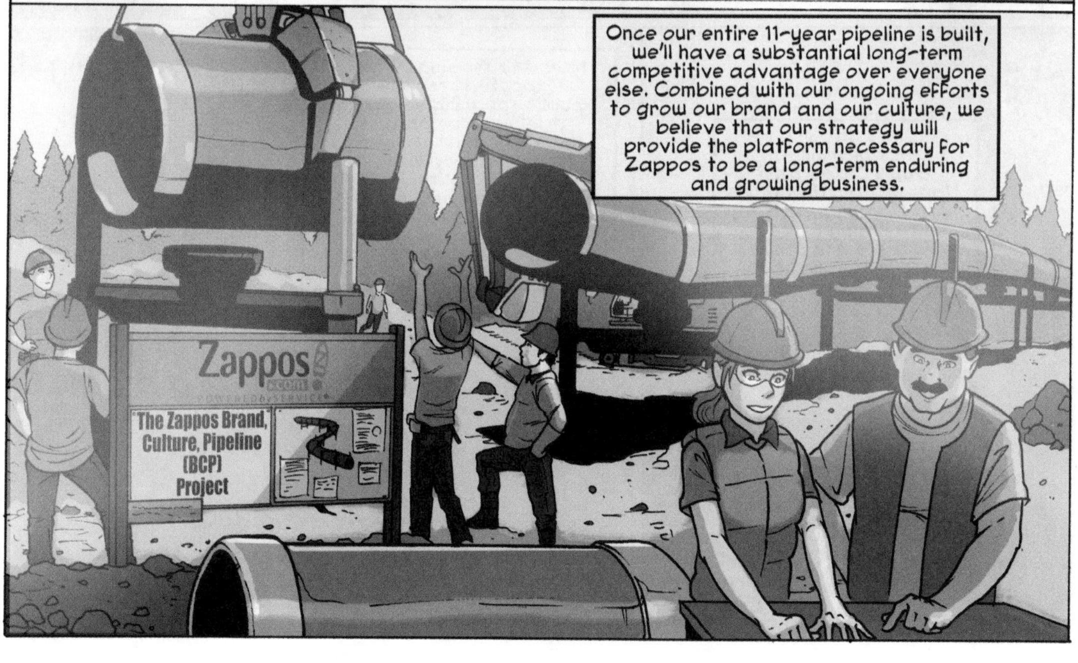
Once our entire 11-year pipeline is built, we'll have a substantial long-term competitive advantage over everyone else. Combined with our ongoing efforts to grow our brand and our culture, we believe that our strategy will provide the platform necessary for Zappos to be a long-term enduring and growing business.
Zappos
The Zappos Brand, Culture, Pipeline (BCP) Project

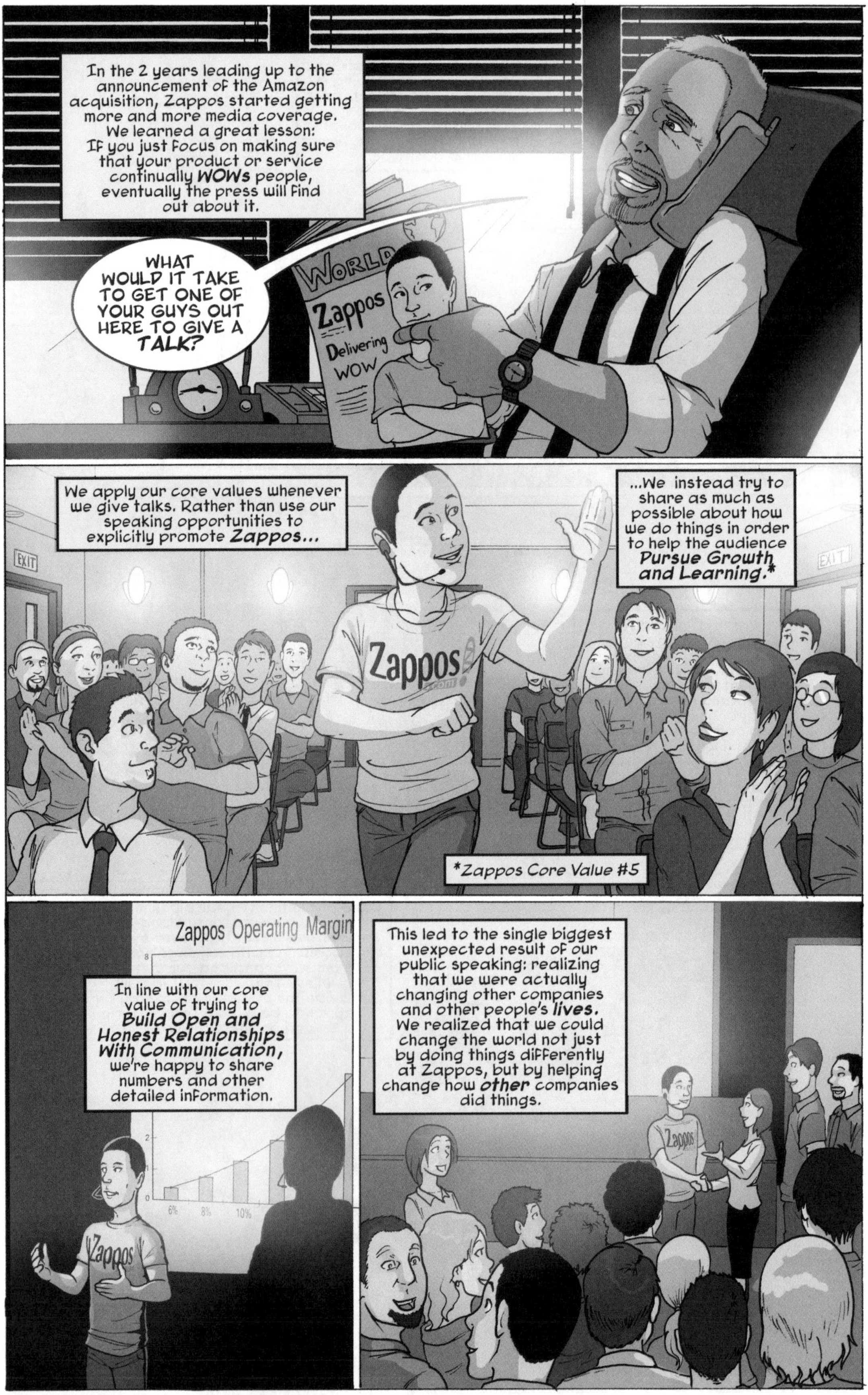
In the 2 years leading up to the announcement of the Amazon acquisition, Zappos started getting more and more media coverage. We learned a great lesson: If you just focus on making sure that your product or service continually **WOWs** people, eventually the press will find out about it.
WORLD
Zappos
Delivering WOW
WHAT WOULD IT TAKE TO GET ONE OF YOUR GUYS OUT HERE TO GIVE A ***TALK?***
We apply our core values whenever we give talks. Rather than use our speaking opportunities to explicitly promote ***Zappos...***
...We instead try to share as much as possible about how we do things in order to help the audience ***Pursue Growth and Learning.****
EXIT
EXIT
Zappos .com
**Zappos Core Value #5*
Zappos Operating Margin
In line with our core value of trying to ***Build Open and Honest Relationships With Communication,*** we're happy to share numbers and other detailed information.
6%
8%
10%
Zappos
This led to the single biggest unexpected result of our public speaking: realizing that we were actually changing other companies and other people's ***lives.*** We realized that we could change the world not just by doing things differently at Zappos, but by helping change how ***other*** companies did things.
Zappos

BUSINESS / SELF-HELP

Books

30% OFF SALE!

EXIT

HISTORY / BIOGRAPHY

BUSINESS

We did not invent the idea that having a vision that had a higher purpose was important.

We did not invent the idea that having a strong culture and core values was important.

GOOD TO GREAT
JIM COLLINS

TRIBAL LEADERSHIP
How Successful Groups form Great Organizations
Dave Logan & John King

DELIVERING Happiness
Zappos

But through tours, the culture book, public speaking, Zappos Insights, Zappos Insights Live, Twitter, and our blogs, we found ourselves in a unique position: We had scaled our business from nothing to over $1 billion in gross merchandise sales in less than 10 years, we had a strong set of integrated core values, and our culture of being open and honest and pursuing growth and learning was leading us to share, rather than hoard all the corporate knowledge and learning we had accumulated over the years.

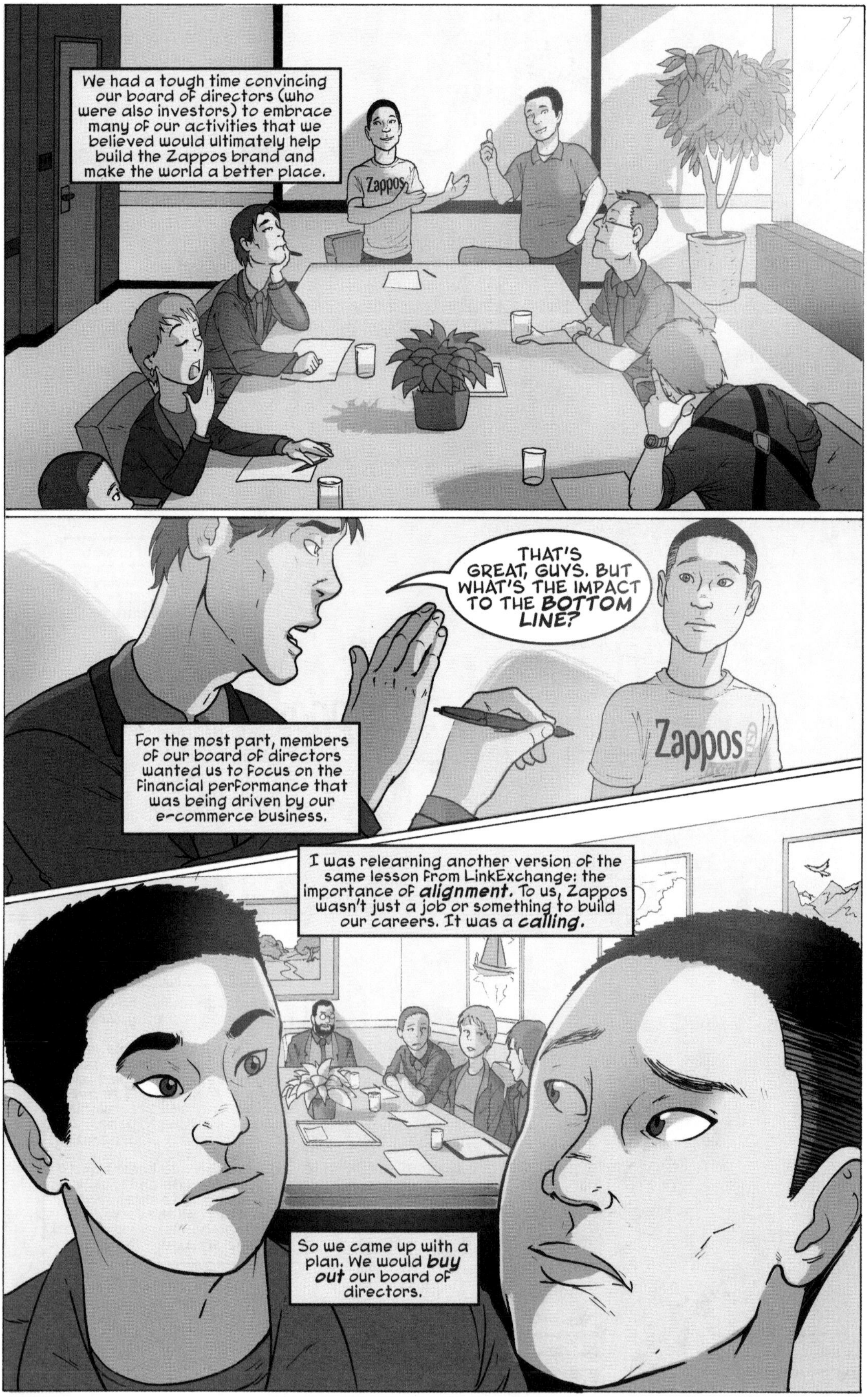
We had a tough time convincing our board of directors (who were also investors) to embrace many of our activities that we believed would ultimately help build the Zappos brand and make the world a better place.
Zappos
THAT'S GREAT, GUYS. BUT WHAT'S THE IMPACT TO THE BOTTOM LINE?
Zappos
For the most part, members of our board of directors wanted us to focus on the financial performance that was being driven by our e-commerce business.
I was relearning another version of the same lesson from LinkExchange: the importance of alignment. To us, Zappos wasn't just a job or something to build our careers. It was a calling.
So we came up with a plan. We would buy out our board of directors.

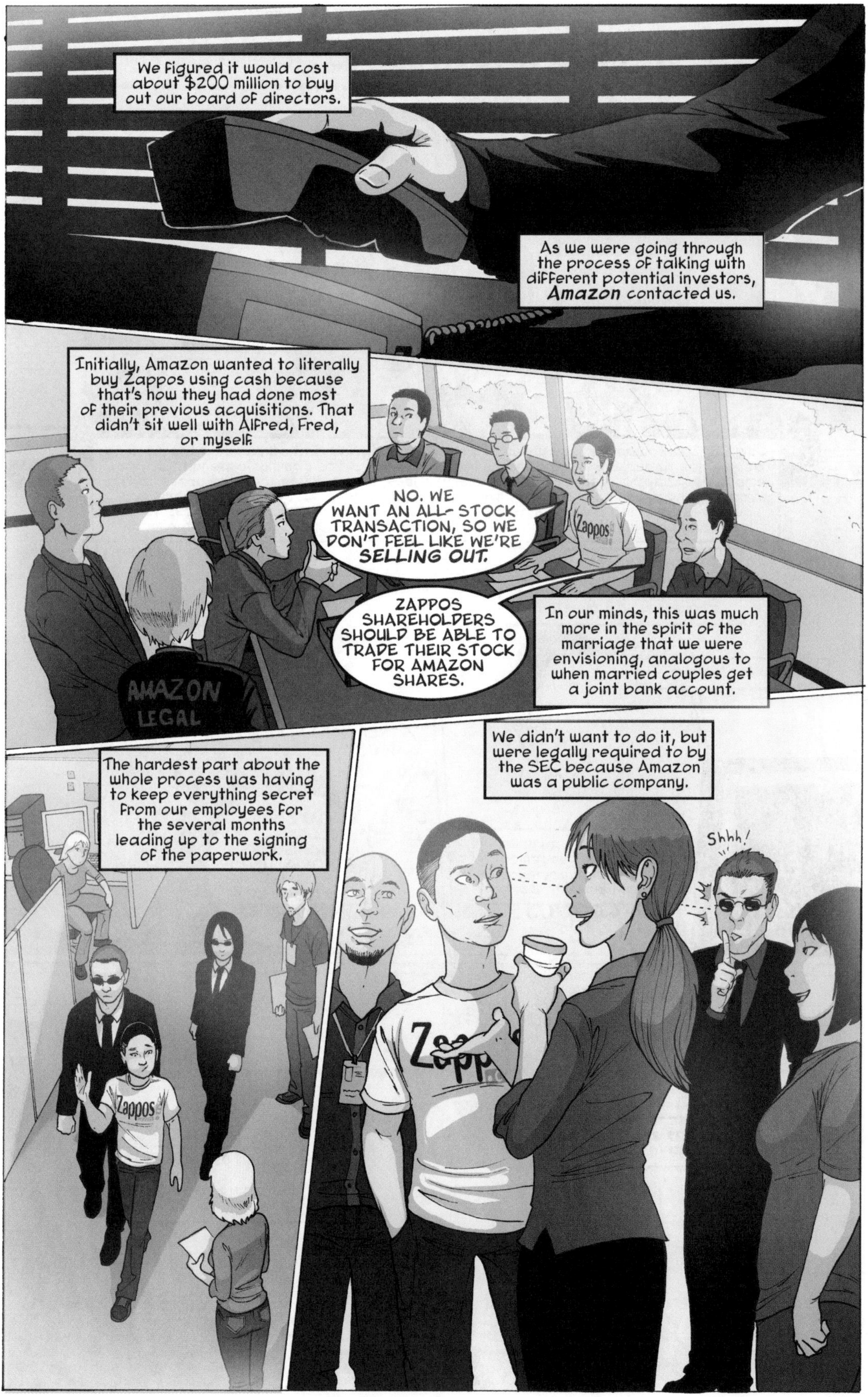

We figured it would cost about $200 million to buy out our board of directors.
As we were going through the process of talking with different potential investors, Amazon contacted us.
Initially, Amazon wanted to literally buy Zappos using cash because that's how they had done most of their previous acquisitions. That didn't sit well with Alfred, Fred, or myself.
NO. WE WANT AN ALL-STOCK TRANSACTION, SO WE DON'T FEEL LIKE WE'RE SELLING OUT.
ZAPPOS SHAREHOLDERS SHOULD BE ABLE TO TRADE THEIR STOCK FOR AMAZON SHARES.
In our minds, this was much more in the spirit of the marriage that we were envisioning, analogous to when married couples get a joint bank account.
AMAZON LEGAL
Zappos
The hardest part about the whole process was having to keep everything secret from our employees for the several months leading up to the signing of the paperwork.
We didn't want to do it, but were legally required to by the SEC because Amazon was a public company.
Shhh!
Zappos
Zappos

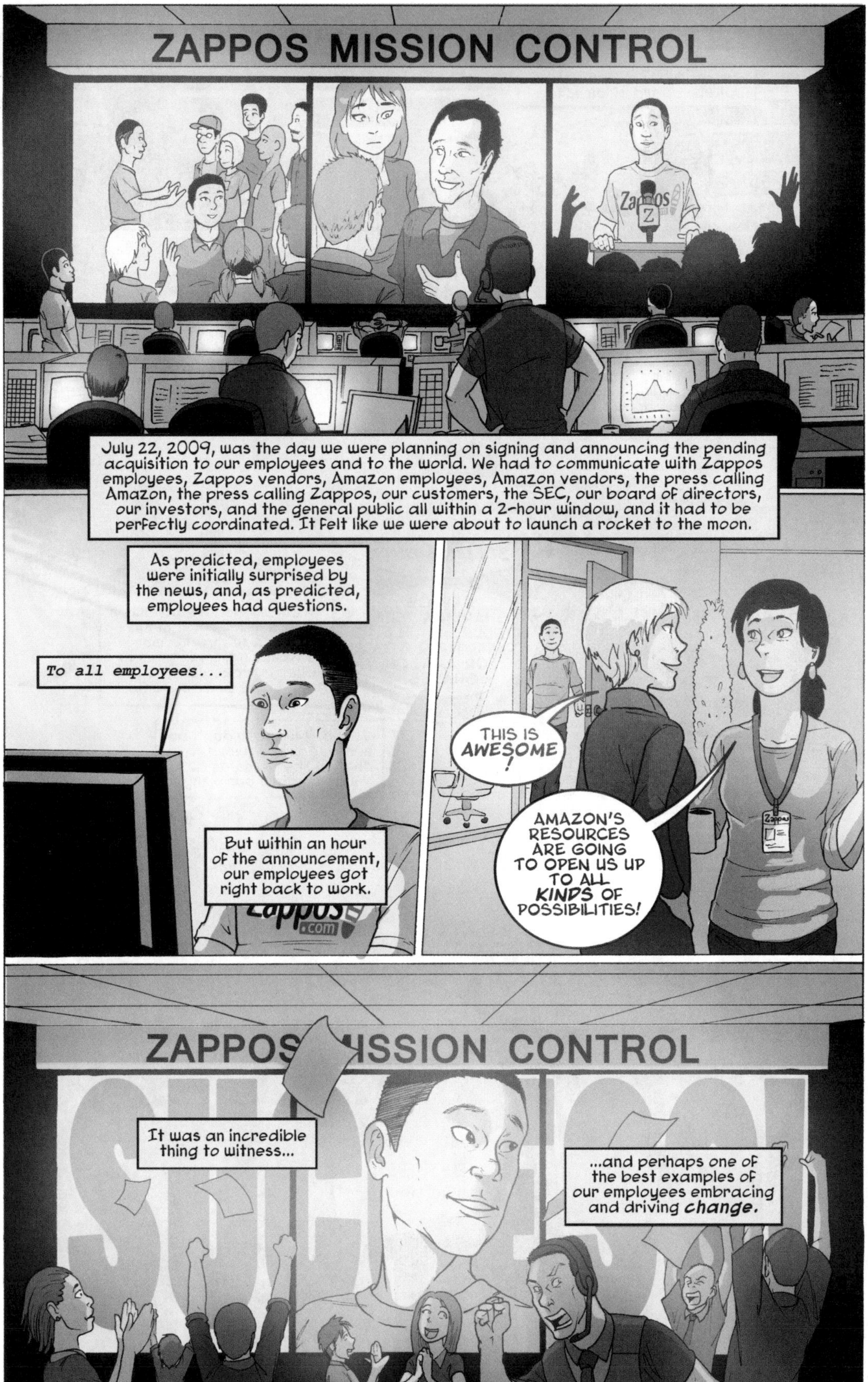
ZAPPOS MISSION CONTROL
July 22, 2009, was the day we were planning on signing and announcing the pending acquisition to our employees and to the world. We had to communicate with Zappos employees, Zappos vendors, Amazon employees, Amazon vendors, the press calling Amazon, the press calling Zappos, our customers, the SEC, our board of directors, our investors, and the general public all within a 2-hour window, and it had to be perfectly coordinated. It felt like we were about to launch a rocket to the moon.
As predicted, employees were initially surprised by the news, and, as predicted, employees had questions.
To all employees...
But within an hour of the announcement, our employees got right back to work.
THIS IS AWESOME!
AMAZON'S RESOURCES ARE GOING TO OPEN US UP TO ALL KINDS OF POSSIBILITIES!
It was an incredible thing to witness...
...and perhaps one of the best examples of our employees embracing and driving change.

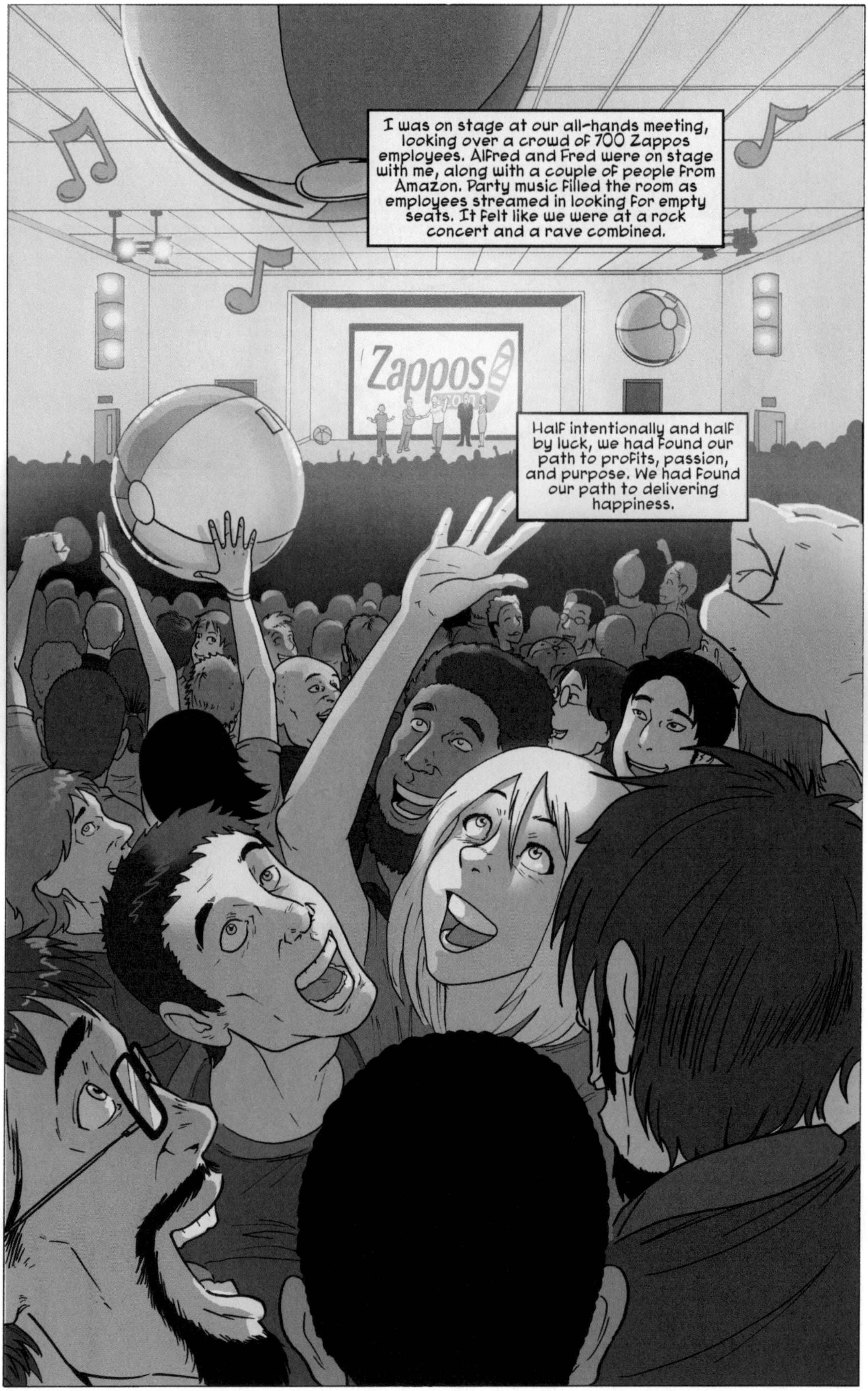
I was on stage at our all-hands meeting, looking over a crowd of 700 Zappos employees. Alfred and Fred were on stage with me, along with a couple of people from Amazon. Party music filled the room as employees streamed in looking for empty seats. It felt like we were at a rock concert and a rave combined.
Zappos
Half intentionally and half by luck, we had found our path to profits, passion, and purpose. We had found our path to delivering happiness.

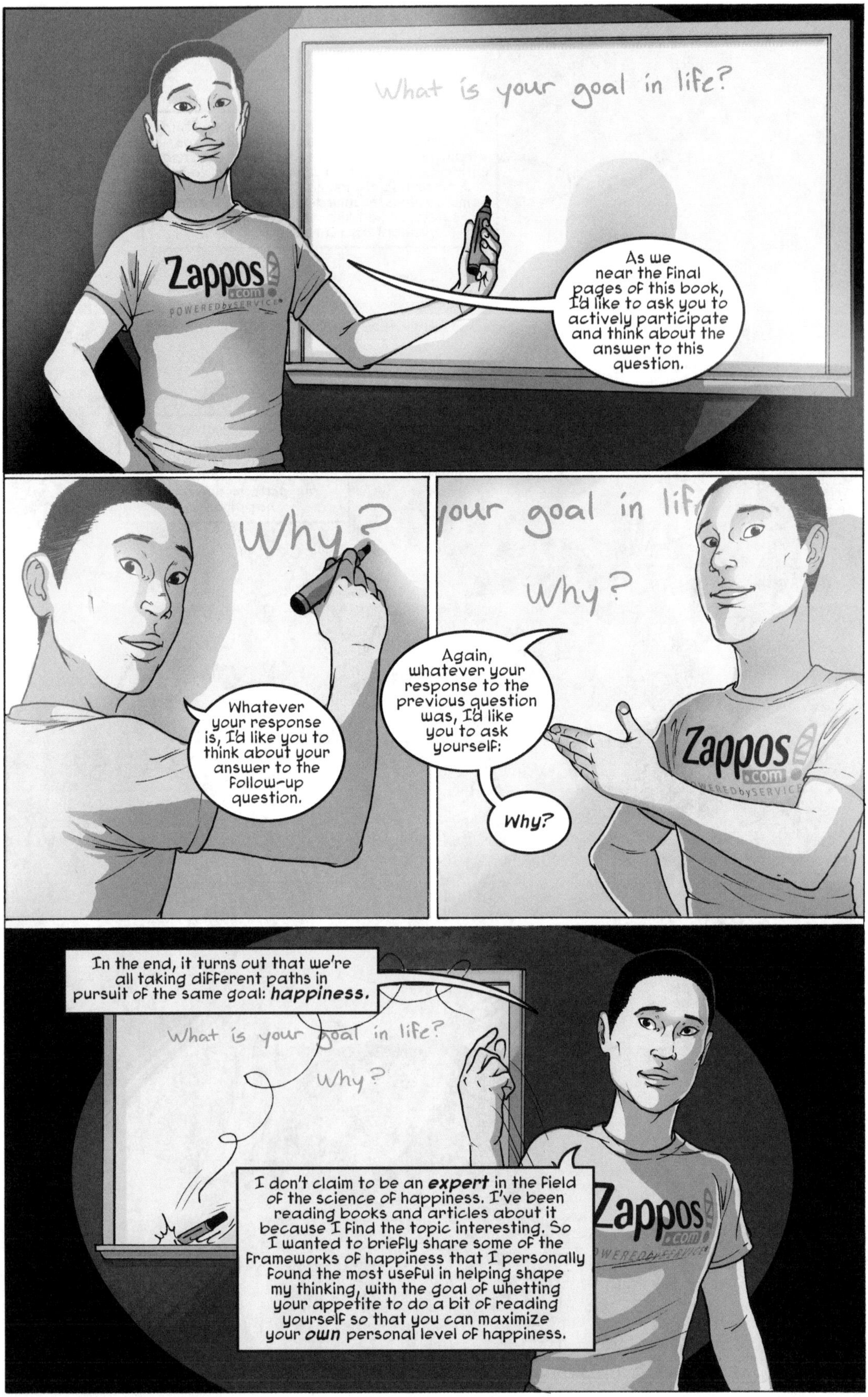
What is your goal in life?
Zappos .com POWERED by SERVICE
As we near the final pages of this book, I'd like to ask you to actively participate and think about the answer to this question.
Why?
Whatever your response is, I'd like you to think about your answer to the follow-up question.
your goal in life
Why?
Again, whatever your response to the previous question was, I'd like you to ask yourself:
Why?
Zappos .com
In the end, it turns out that we're all taking different paths in pursuit of the same goal: happiness.
What is your goal in life?
Why?
I don't claim to be an expert in the field of the science of happiness. I've been reading books and articles about it because I find the topic interesting. So I wanted to briefly share some of the frameworks of happiness that I personally found the most useful in helping shape my thinking, with the goal of whetting your appetite to do a bit of reading yourself so that you can maximize your own personal level of happiness.
Zappos .com

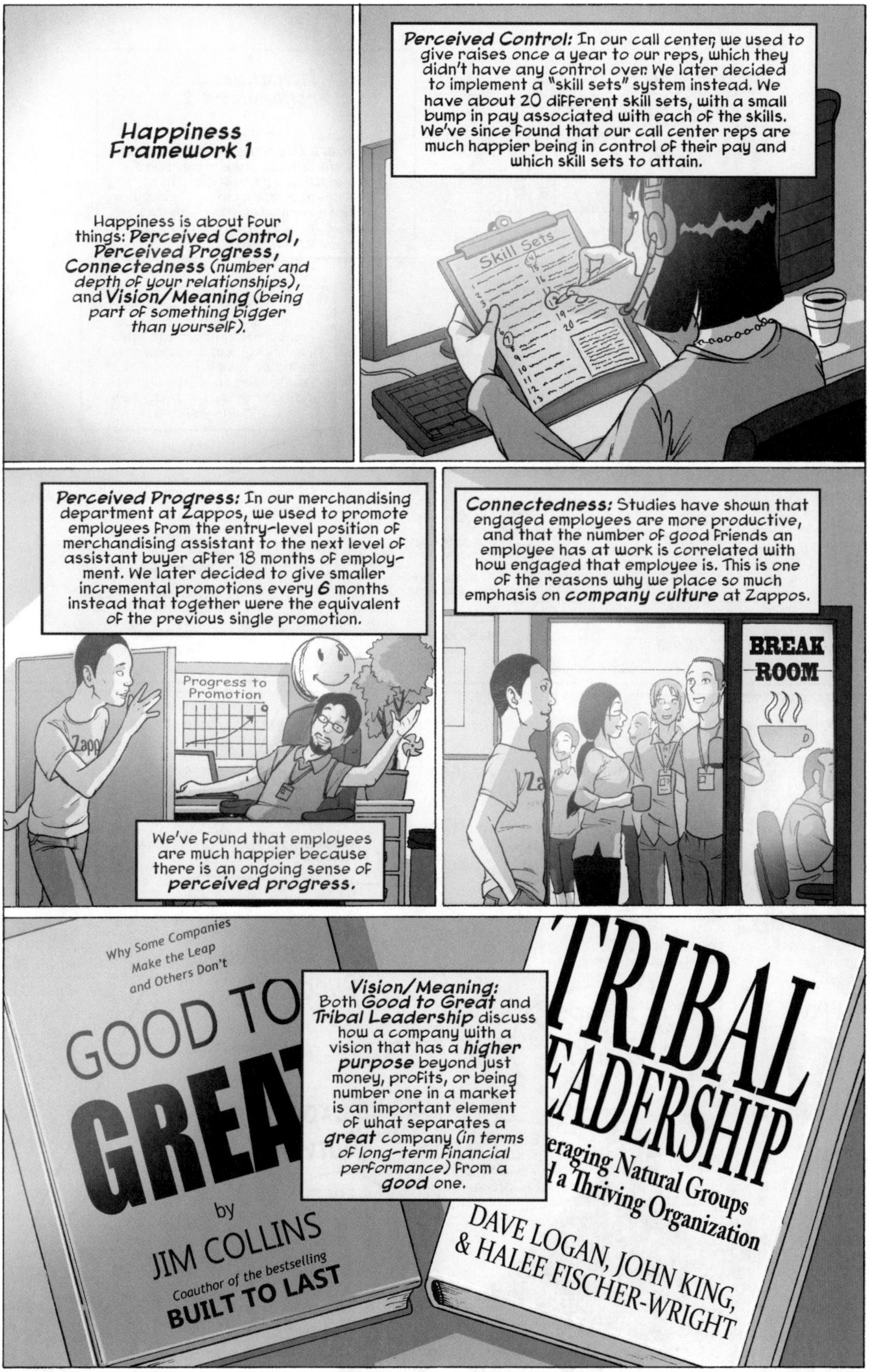
Happiness Framework 1
Happiness is about four things: Perceived Control, Perceived Progress, Connectedness (number and depth of your relationships), and Vision/Meaning (being part of something bigger than yourself).
Perceived Control: In our call center, we used to give raises once a year to our reps, which they didn't have any control over. We later decided to implement a "skill sets" system instead. We have about 20 different skill sets, with a small bump in pay associated with each of the skills. We've since found that our call center reps are much happier being in control of their pay and which skill sets to attain.
Skill Sets
Perceived Progress: In our merchandising department at Zappos, we used to promote employees from the entry-level position of merchandising assistant to the next level of assistant buyer after 18 months of employment. We later decided to give smaller incremental promotions every 6 months instead that together were the equivalent of the previous single promotion.
Progress to Promotion
We've found that employees are much happier because there is an ongoing sense of perceived progress.
Connectedness: Studies have shown that engaged employees are more productive, and that the number of good friends an employee has at work is correlated with how engaged that employee is. This is one of the reasons why we place so much emphasis on company culture at Zappos.
BREAK ROOM
Why Some Companies Make the Leap and Others Don't
GOOD TO
GREAT
by
JIM COLLINS
Coauthor of the bestselling
BUILT TO LAST
Vision/Meaning: Both Good to Great and Tribal Leadership discuss how a company with a vision that has a higher purpose beyond just money, profits, or being number one in a market is an important element of what separates a great company (in terms of long-term financial performance) from a good one.
TRIBAL
EADERSHIP
eraging Natural Groups
d a Thriving Organization
DAVE LOGAN, JOHN KING,
& HALEE FISCHER-WRIGHT

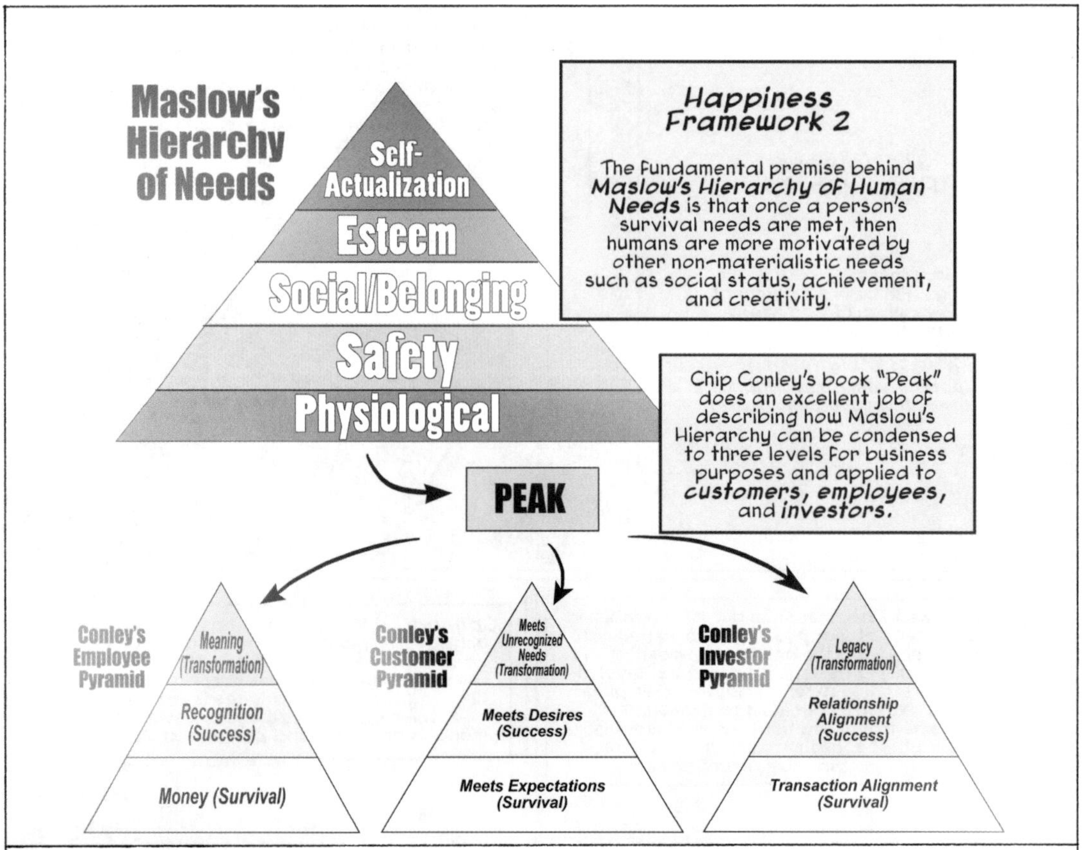
Maslow's Hierarchy of Needs
Self-Actualization
Esteem
Social/Belonging
Safety
Physiological
Happiness Framework 2
The fundamental premise behind *Maslow's Hierarchy of Human Needs* is that once a person's survival needs are met, then humans are more motivated by other non-materialistic needs such as social status, achievement, and creativity.
Chip Conley's book "Peak" does an excellent job of describing how Maslow's Hierarchy can be condensed to three levels for business purposes and applied to *customers, employees,* and *investors.*
PEAK
Conley's Employee Pyramid
Meaning (Transformation)
Recognition (Success)
Money (Survival)
Conley's Customer Pyramid
Meets Unrecognized Needs (Transformation)
Meets Desires (Success)
Meets Expectations (Survival)
Conley's Investor Pyramid
Legacy (Transformation)
Relationship Alignment (Success)
Transaction Alignment (Survival)

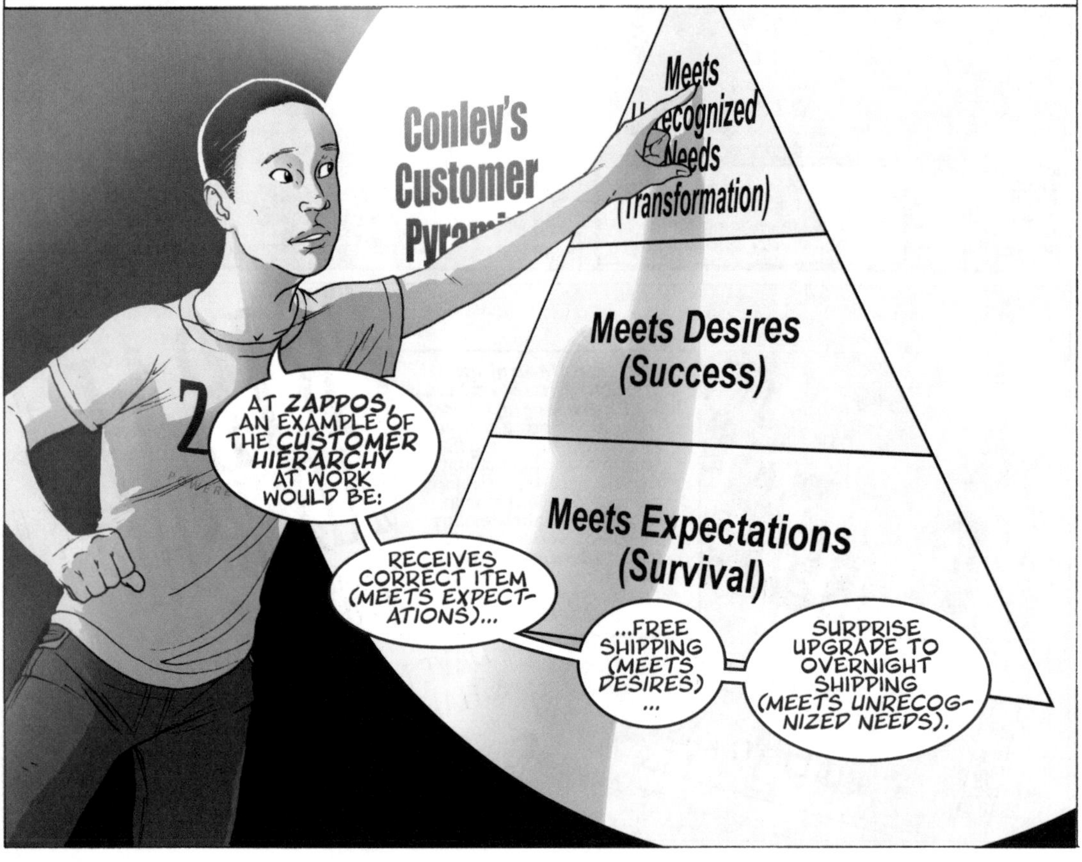
Conley's Customer
Meets
Needs
(Transformation)
Meets Desires (Success)
Meets Expectations (Survival)
AT ZAPPOS, AN EXAMPLE OF THE CUSTOMER HIERARCHY AT WORK WOULD BE:
RECEIVES CORRECT ITEM (MEETS EXPECTATIONS)...
...FREE SHIPPING (MEETS DESIRES) ...
SURPRISE UPGRADE TO OVERNIGHT SHIPPING (MEETS UNRECOGNIZED NEEDS).

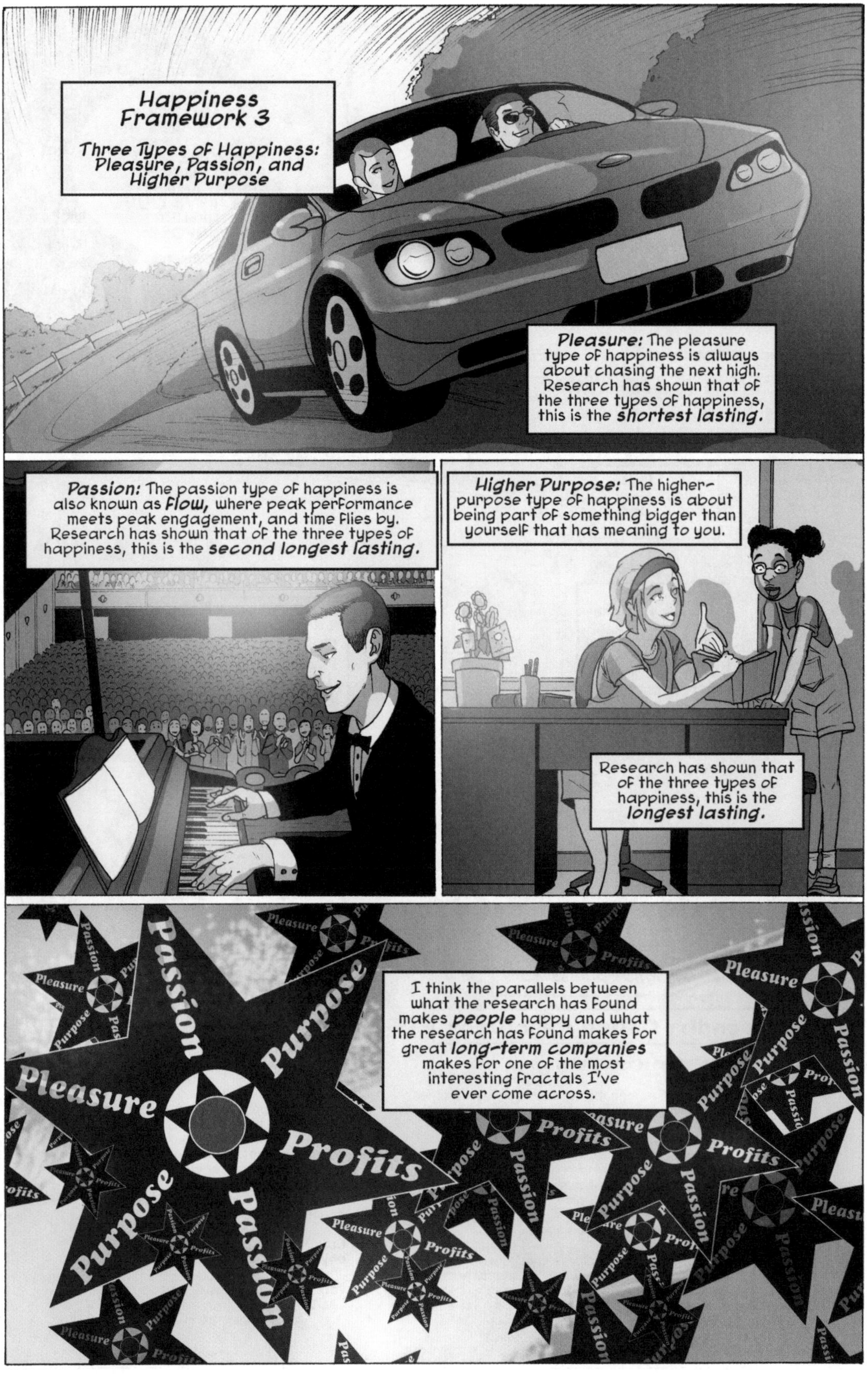
Happiness Framework 3
Three Types of Happiness: Pleasure, Passion, and Higher Purpose
Pleasure: The pleasure type of happiness is always about chasing the next high. Research has shown that of the three types of happiness, this is the shortest lasting.
Passion: The passion type of happiness is also known as flow, where peak performance meets peak engagement, and time flies by. Research has shown that of the three types of happiness, this is the second longest lasting.
Higher Purpose: The higher-purpose type of happiness is about being part of something bigger than yourself that has meaning to you.
Research has shown that of the three types of happiness, this is the longest lasting.
I think the parallels between what the research has found makes people happy and what the research has found makes for great long-term companies makes for one of the most interesting fractals I've ever come across.
Pleasure
Passion
Purpose
Profits

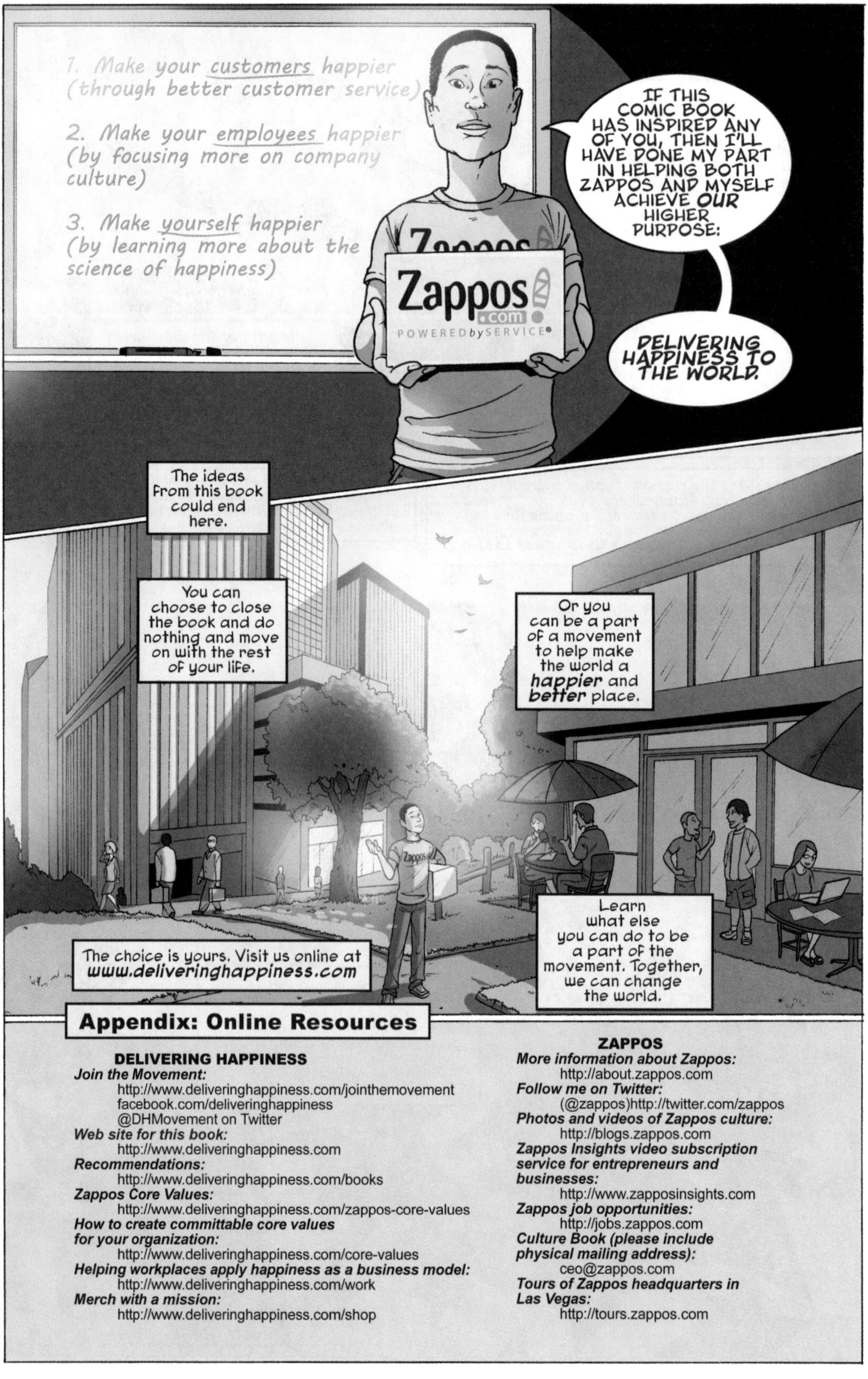
1. Make your customers happier (through better customer service)
2. Make your employees happier (by focusing more on company culture)
3. Make yourself happier (by learning more about the science of happiness)
Zappos.com POWERED by SERVICE®
IF THIS COMIC BOOK HAS INSPIRED ANY OF YOU, THEN I'LL HAVE DONE MY PART IN HELPING BOTH ZAPPOS AND MYSELF ACHIEVE OUR HIGHER PURPOSE:
DELIVERING HAPPINESS TO THE WORLD.
The ideas from this book could end here.
You can choose to close the book and do nothing and move on with the rest of your life.
Or you can be a part of a movement to help make the world a happier and better place.
The choice is yours. Visit us online at www.deliveringhappiness.com
Learn what else you can do to be a part of the movement. Together, we can change the world.

Appendix: Online Resources

DELIVERING HAPPINESS

Join the Movement:
http://www.deliveringhappiness.com/jointhemovement
facebook.com/deliveringhappiness
@DHMovement on Twitter

Web site for this book:
http://www.deliveringhappiness.com

Recommendations:
http://www.deliveringhappiness.com/books

Zappos Core Values:
http://www.deliveringhappiness.com/zappos-core-values

How to create committable core values for your organization:
http://www.deliveringhappiness.com/core-values

Helping workplaces apply happiness as a business model:
http://www.deliveringhappiness.com/work

Merch with a mission:
http://www.deliveringhappiness.com/shop

ZAPPOS

More information about Zappos:
http://about.zappos.com

Follow me on Twitter:
(@zappos)http://twitter.com/zappos

Photos and videos of Zappos culture:
http://blogs.zappos.com

Zappos Insights video subscription service for entrepreneurs and businesses:
http://www.zapposinsights.com

Zappos job opportunities:
http://jobs.zappos.com

Culture Book (please include physical mailing address):
ceo@zappos.com

Tours of Zappos headquarters in Las Vegas:
http://tours.zappos.com

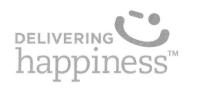

DELIVERING happiness™

Inspire and Be Inspired.™

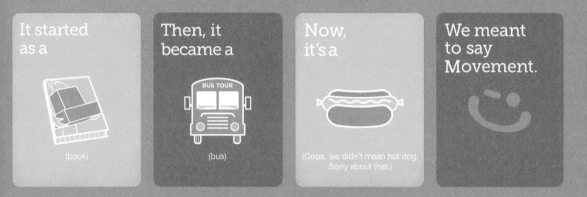

It started as a

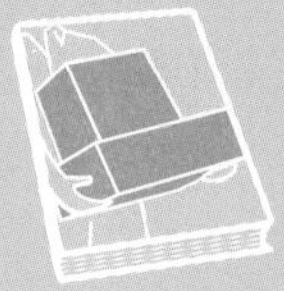

(book)

Then, it became a

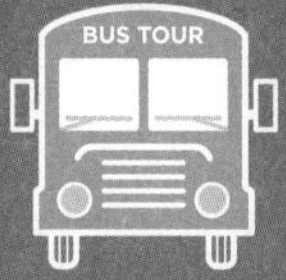
BUS TOUR

(bus)

Now, it's a

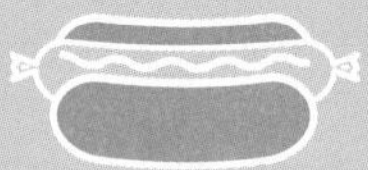

(Oops, we didn't mean hot dog. Sorry about that.)

We meant to say Movement.

We all want to be happy. But as research shows, it turns out we're super bad at predicting what will bring us lasting joy. (Surprise, it's not money or beauty.) Simply put, we all want to be part of something bigger than ourselves. To find a higher purpose.

That's where Delivering Happiness comes in.
We're a movement that spreads good vibes. At home. At work. In the community. We're nudging the world to a happier place—one smile at a time. Backed by scientific sense, business sense and common sense, we know that true satisfaction in life is what really matters. So come along for the ride and join the Movement.

Inspire and Be Inspired.

deliveringhappiness.com

twitter.com/dhmovement

facebook.com/deliveringhappiness

Merch with a Mission

When's the last time you went shopping and came home
with a global movement?

The goods in our shop are on a mission to make a difference.
To share good vibes. To spark conversation.
To fuel what Delivering Happiness is doing every day—
inspiring people to spread happiness around the globe.
When you wear DH gear, you're joining our team and helping
us nudge the world to a happier place.

 →  →

Outfit yourself in   100% of profits   Supports events and programs
DH goods and gear   from your purchase   to deliver happiness
                                                     around the world

deliveringhappiness.com/shop

We make happy...work.™

If your business put on a mood ring, what color would it be?

A third of our lives is spent at work. So whether you're the CEO, managing a team or answering the phones, why not make it a place where everyone feels great?

The most successful companies recognize they have to bust out of the cubicles, throw open the doors of the corner offices, and cultivate an environment of trust and transparency. They understand the path of retention, productivity and profit is born from an inspiring corporate culture with purpose as its core and happiness as a business model. And they know a satisfying life is the best gig of all.

So work with us—
we'll help you make a career out of being happy.

deliveringhappinessatwork.com

The book that inspired the comic…

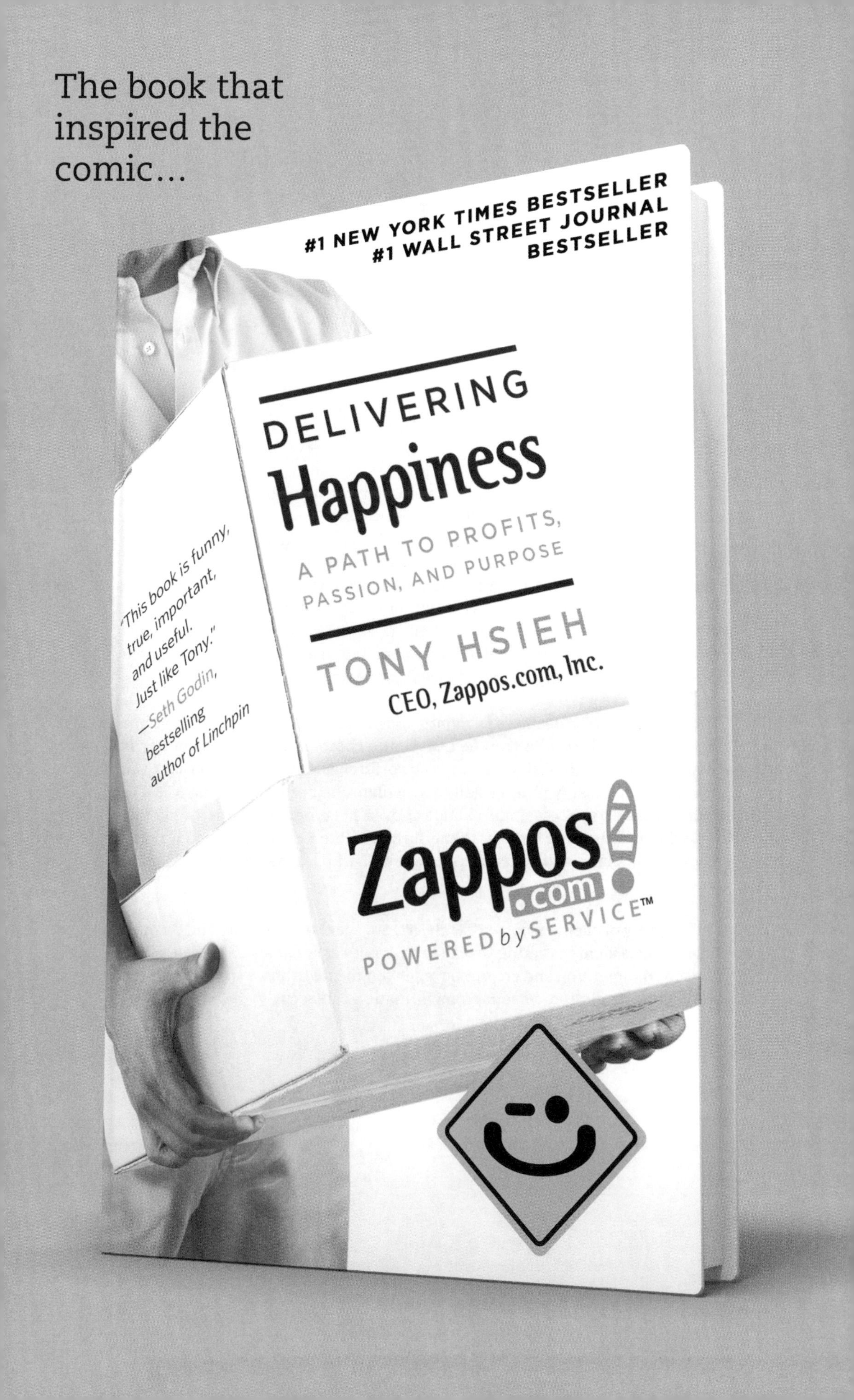
#1 NEW YORK TIMES BESTSELLER
#1 WALL STREET JOURNAL BESTSELLER
DELIVERING
Happiness
A PATH TO PROFITS, PASSION, AND PURPOSE
TONY HSIEH
CEO, Zappos.com, Inc.
"This book is funny, true, important, and useful. Just like Tony."
—Seth Godin, bestselling author of Linchpin
Zappos.com
POWERED by SERVICE™

round table companies

about round table companies

Round Table Companies uses a filmmaker's approach to storytelling to inform, educate, and inspire readers. Trusted by *New York Times* bestselling authors Marshall Goldsmith, Chris Anderson, Tony Hsieh, and Robert Cialdini, RTC's approach to creating high quality content eliminates the traditional publishing gatekeepers and allows thought leaders to engage in a fully collaborative team approach to distilling their ideas into either word based or illustrated formats. Whether working with a first time author, or a seasoned veteran, RTC surrounds each author with an entire staff of professionals who understand how to create an emotional and engaging experience for readers.

While 25% of RTC's business is repurposing best-selling non-fiction content in the illustrated form of graphic novels, the company's bread and butter is thought leaders and businesses with powerful messages who either lack the time or the necessary writing skill to articulate their wisdom. Using RTC's in depth interview process and full staff of over 20 storytelling experts, clients' powerful messages are brought to the surface in their own words and eventually used to shape a full manuscript that is then packaged by the RTC team for distribution.

The majority of clients who work with RTC engage them for years and on multiple projects, demonstrating that the company's core values of brilliance, joy, honesty, momentum, and growth have proven to create an atmosphere where storytelling magic and personal transformation can occur.

Check out these
other great titles
from
Round Table Comics!

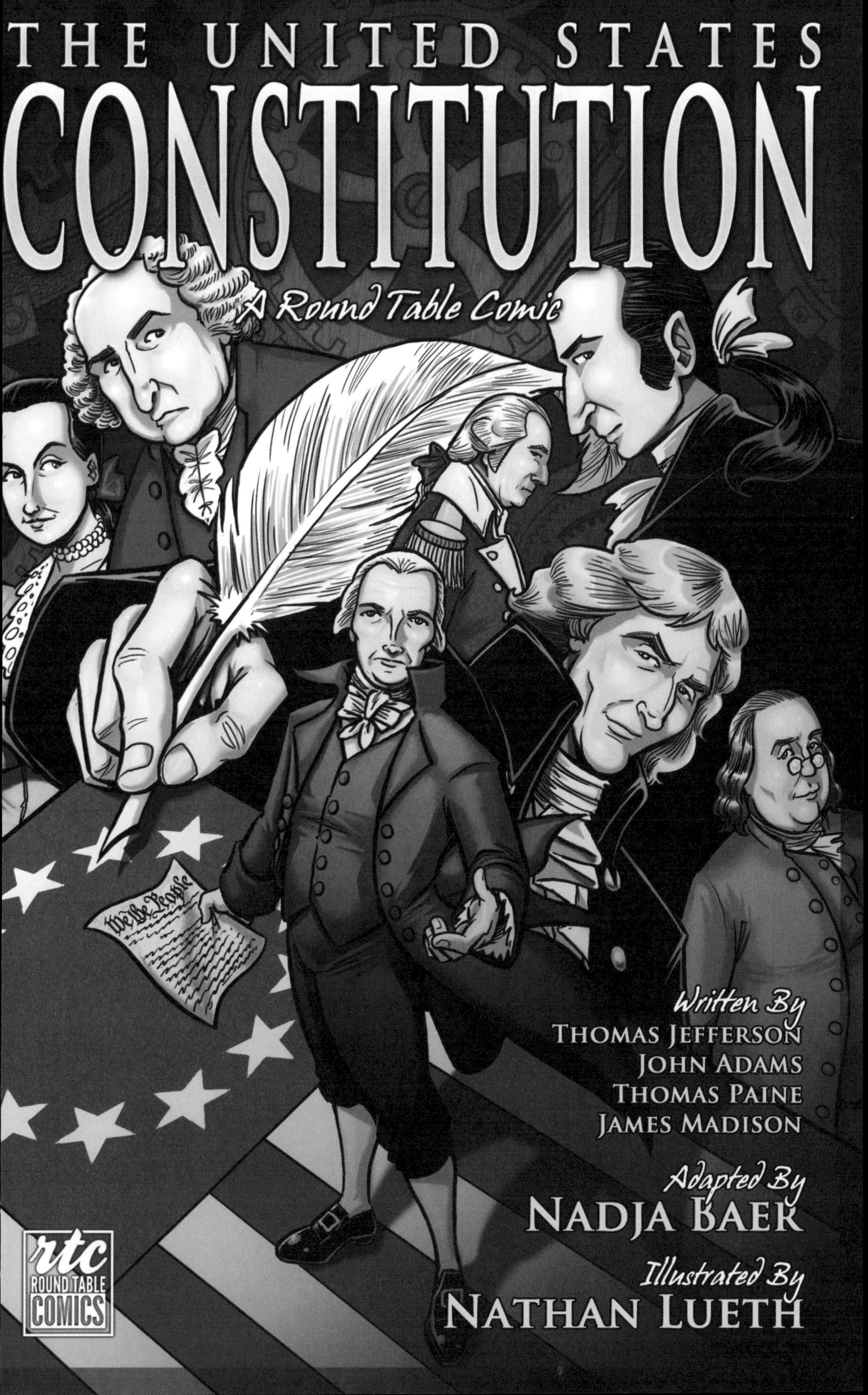
THE UNITED STATES
CONSTITUTION
A Round Table Comic
We the People
Written By
THOMAS JEFFERSON
JOHN ADAMS
THOMAS PAINE
JAMES MADISON
Adapted By
NADJA BAEK
Illustrated By
NATHAN LUETH
rtc
ROUND TABLE
COMICS

HOW SMART COMPANIES GET PEOPLE TALKING

WORD OF MOUTH MARKETING

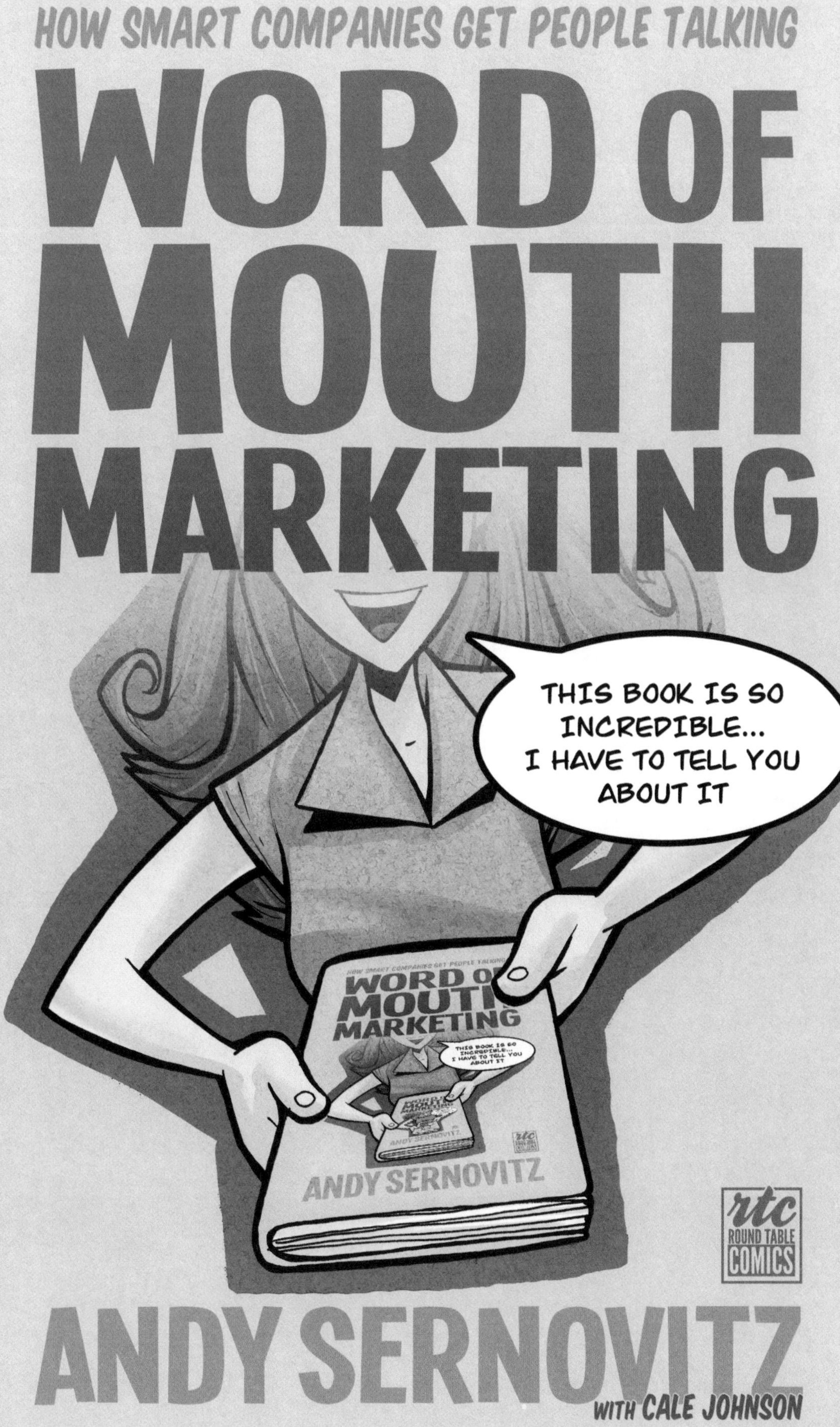
THIS BOOK IS SO INCREDIBLE... I HAVE TO TELL YOU ABOUT IT
MARKETING
ANDY SERNOVITZ

rtc ROUND TABLE COMICS

ANDY SERNOVITZ

WITH CALE JOHNSON

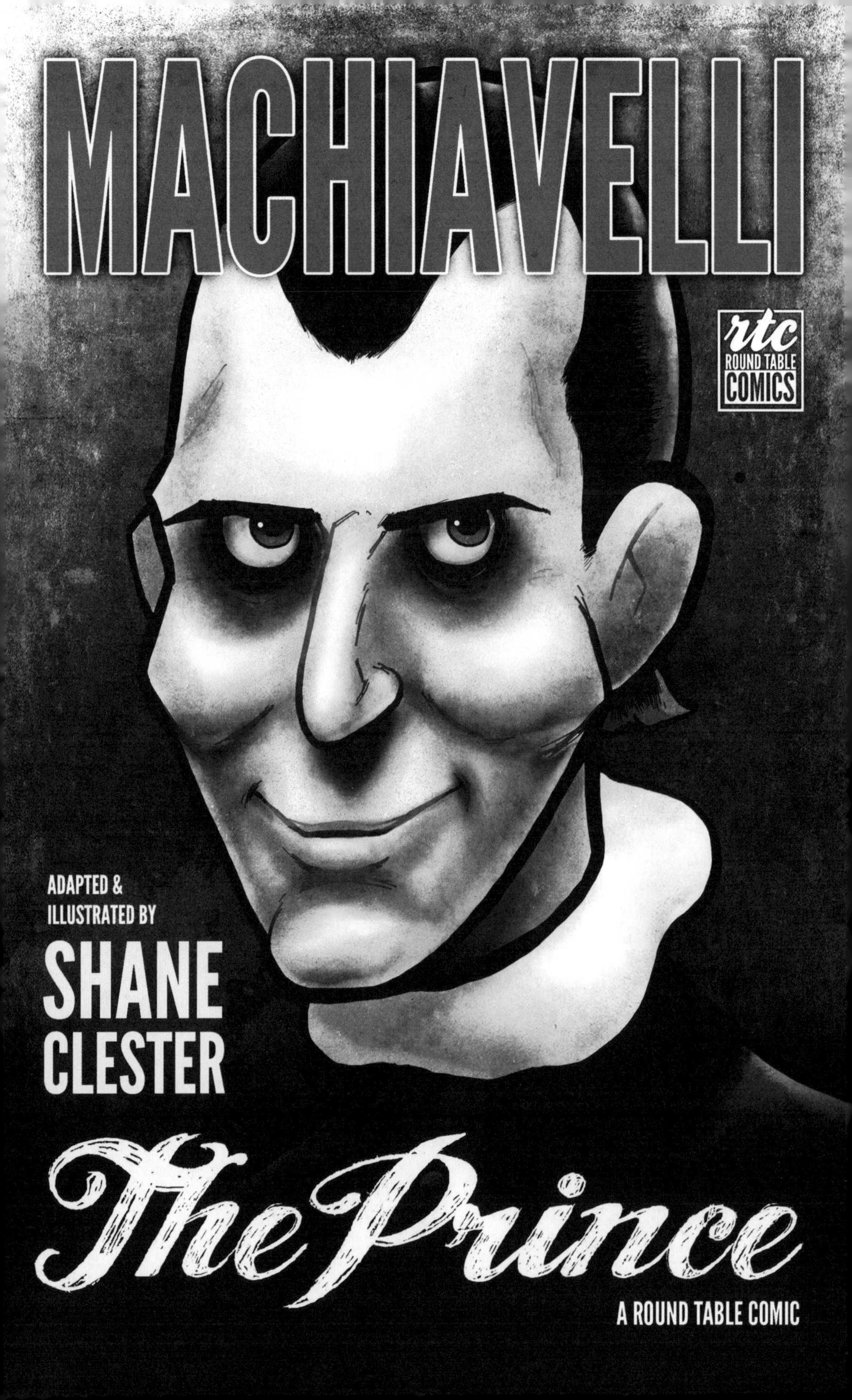
MACHIAVELLI
rtc
ROUND TABLE
COMICS
ADAPTED &
ILLUSTRATED BY
SHANE
CLESTER
The Prince
A ROUND TABLE COMIC

Based on the book *From the Barrio to the Board Room*

Mi Barrio

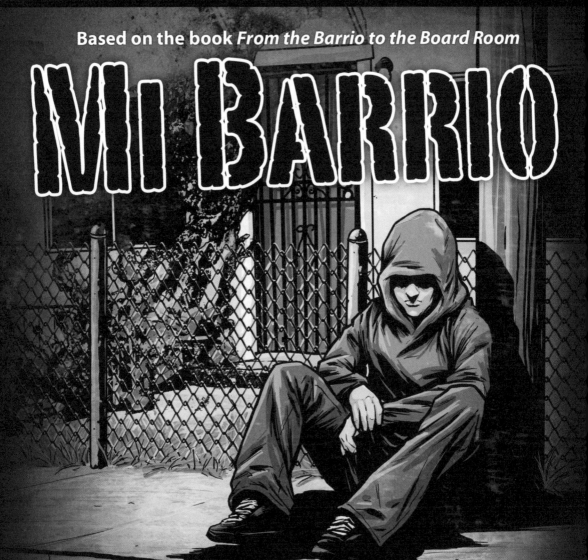

"DON'T LET WHERE YOU CAME FROM DICTATE WHO YOU ARE,
BUT LET IT BE PART OF WHO YOU BECOME."

Robert Renteria

As told to **Corey Michael Blake**

Illustrated by **Shane Clester**

Free Curriculum Available

HOW SUCCESSFUL PEOPLE BECOME EVEN MORE SUCCESSFUL

WHAT GOT YOU HERE WON'T GET YOU THERE

DISCOVER THE 20 WORKPLACE HABITS THAT YOU NEED TO BREAK

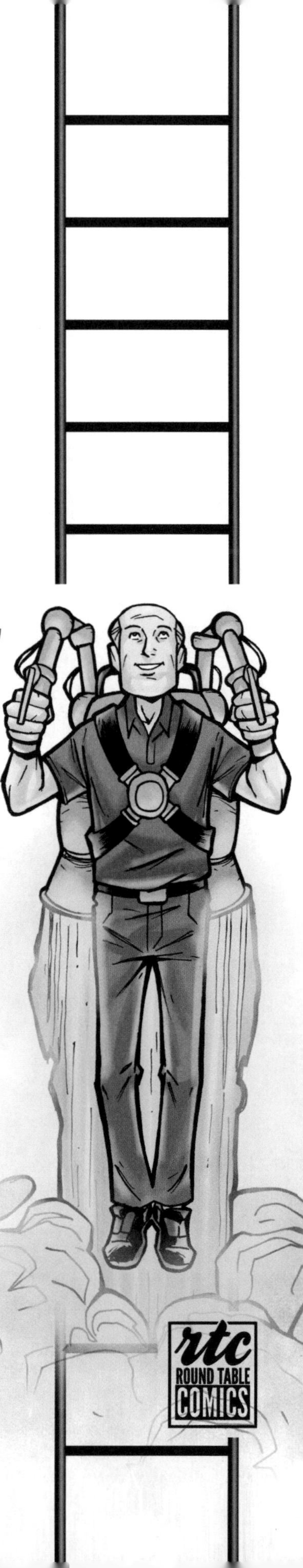

MARSHALL GOLDSMITH

WITH MARK REITER

ILLUSTRATED BY

SHANE CLESTER

RTC ROUND TABLE COMICS

www.roundtablecompanies.com